Soft Pastel

WITH KEN GOLDMAN, MARILYN GRAME, AND WILLIAM SCHNEIDER

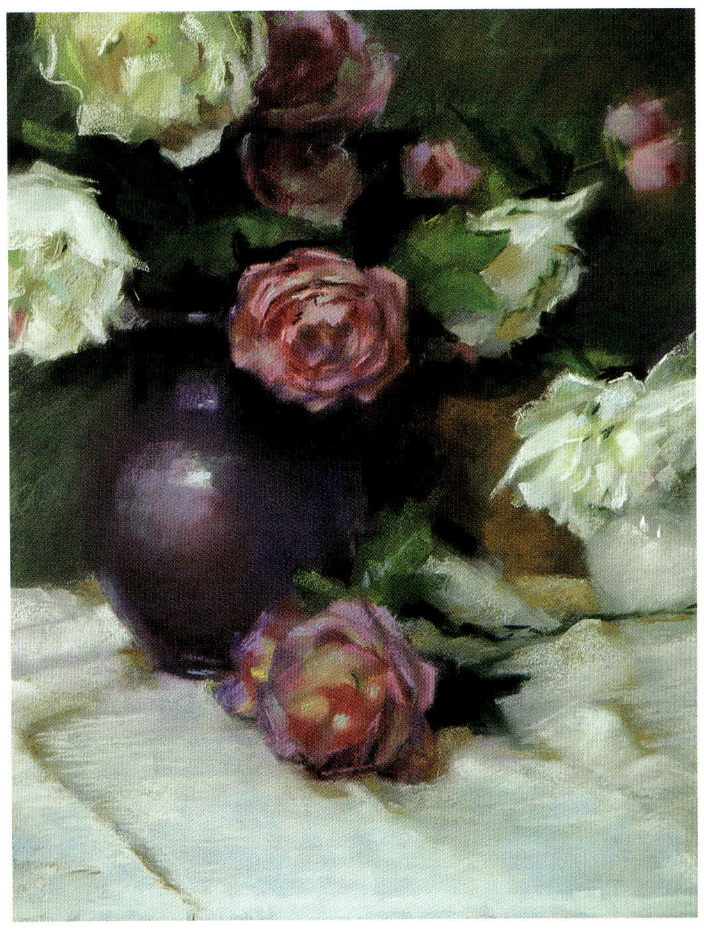

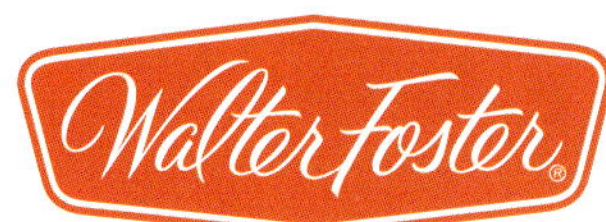

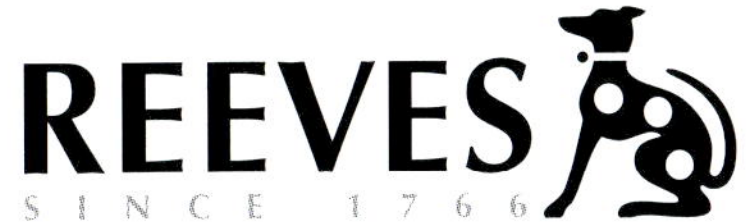

Contents

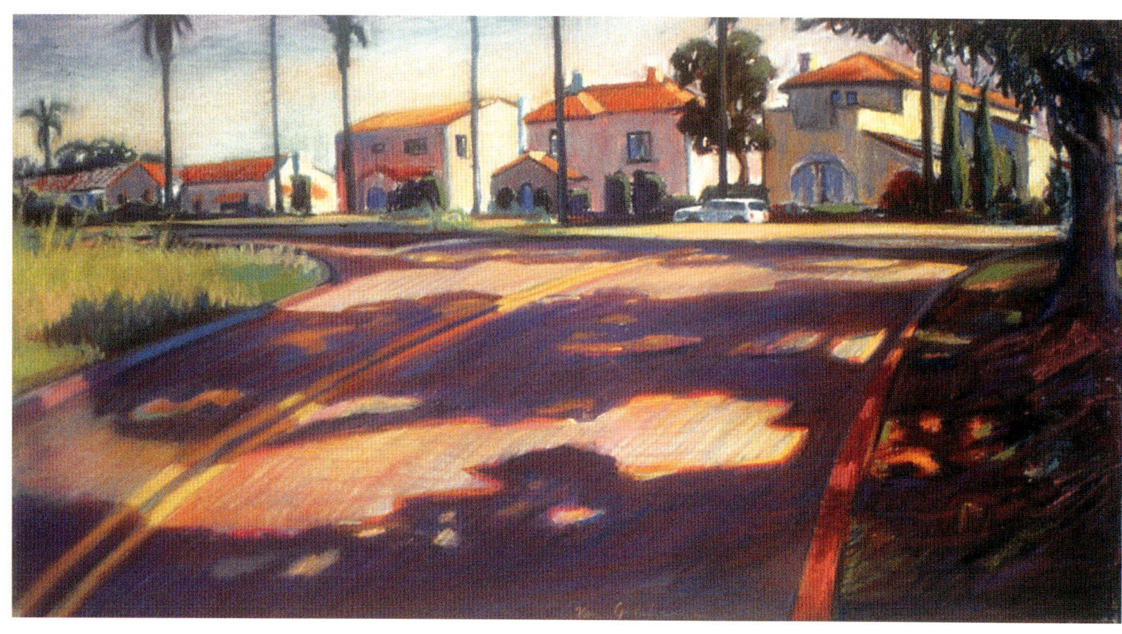

Introduction

Pastel is a wonderful painting medium. The colors can be rich and vibrant or soft and subdued, and you can create many interesting and varied textures by blending and layering pastels. By twisting the pastel stick or using the tip instead of the side, you can produce anything from precise lines to broad strokes. And because it's dry to begin with, the color won't change after it has been applied; nor will it fade, crack, or yellow over time.

In this book, three accomplished pastel artists will share their personal tips and methods for painting a number of captivating soft pastel subjects—from landscapes and still lifes to animals and portraits. Each artist guides you step by step through the lessons, starting with initial sketches and ending with the finishing details. You will also learn a variety of techniques that will give you a new appreciation of the medium, inspire you to explore the creative possibilities that pastel has to offer, and allow you to create your own works of fine art!

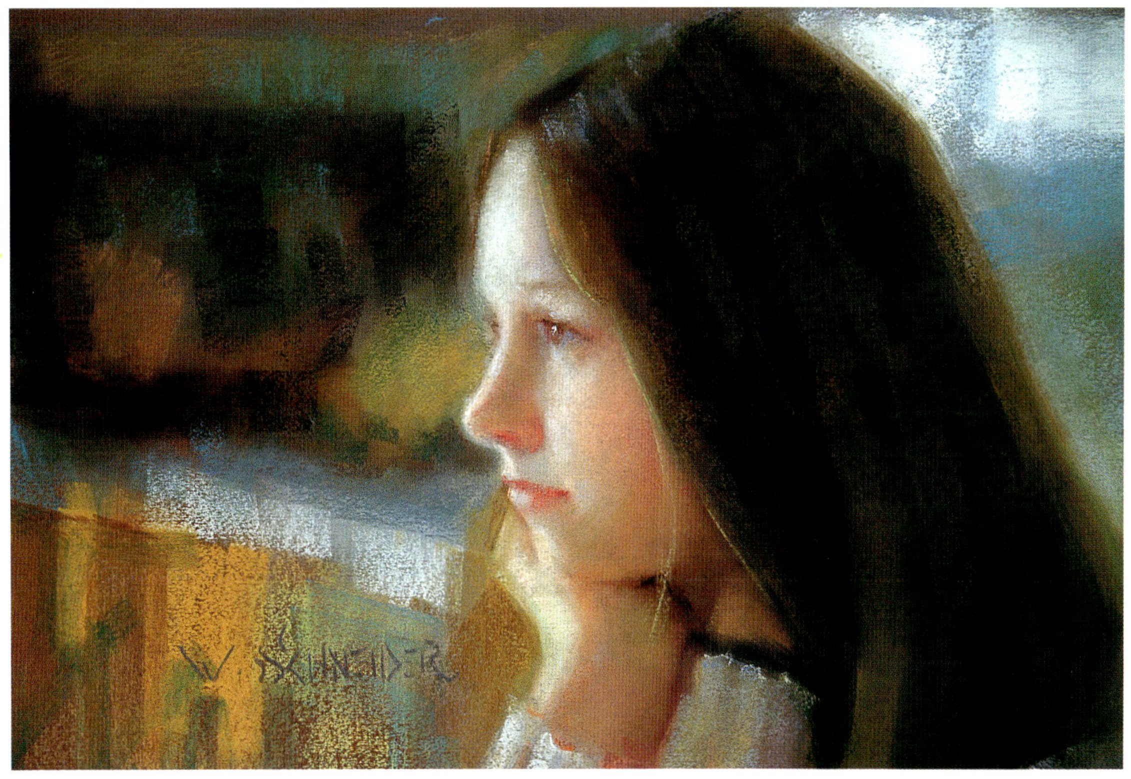

Tools and Materials

Pastel Supplies

You don't need many supplies to paint in pastel; unlike oil or acrylic paints, this medium doesn't require additives or brushes. All you really need is a set of pastels and a variety of papers (or *supports*). And if you add a few additional materials described on these pages, you'll be ready to explore the range of possibilities pastel has to offer.

Soft Pastels

Pastels are available in several forms—including oil pastels and hard, clay-based pastel sticks and pastel pencils—but chalklike soft pastels are a popular choice and are the type used for the projects in this book. These sticks produce a beautiful, velvety texture and are easy to blend with your fingers or a cloth. If you are a beginner, you may want to purchase a preselected set of colors. Reeves offers three convenient sets, each in a different quantity. When purchasing pastels, keep in mind that pastel colors are mixed on the paper as you paint, rather than premixed on a palette. Therefore try to buy a wide range of colors in various values (lights, mediums, and darks; see page 13) so you will always have the color you want readily at hand.

Pastel Supports

The texture and color of the paper you choose to paint on will affect your results. Because of the delicate nature of soft pastels, you need a paper that has some *tooth,* or grain, for the pigment to stick to. A rough support, such as pumice board or sanded paper (both made especially for pastel application), will "break up" the applied strokes and create texture, while a smoother surface, such as velour, canvas, or watercolor paper, will make the unbroken colors appear more intense. Pastel supports are also available in a variety of colors; you can choose a color that offers a contrasting background tone or one that is in the same color range as your subject. (For more on using colored supports, see pages 11, 18, and 26–31.)

Other Necessities

In addition to pastels and papers, a few other tools will come in handy as you paint. Use scissors to trim your supports and vine charcoal to sketch your subjects. (Charcoal is easy to erase and can be painted over with pastel.) A sandpaper block works well as a sharpener, and a razor blade is great for breaking the pastels cleanly. Sometimes you may wish to stroke over your base coat with denatured alcohol on a soft brush to wash the color thoroughly into the paper. You will also need tools for blending, such as a foam brush, a soft rag, or a paper blending stump. (See page 10 for more information on blending.) You may want to purchase spray fixative (see page 11) and acrylic or watercolor paints and brushes for underpaintings. And to protect your finished artwork from smearing, always store your pastel paintings between a board and a cover sheet: Purchase artist's tissue paper by the roll and cut it to fit your painting; then affix the paper to the back of the support with low-tack artist's tape.

Work Space

Your work area can be an elaborate studio or just a corner in a room, but two elements are absolutely essential: comfort and good lighting. Natural light is best, and you'll want to work in a place where you'll have few distractions. Also include a supportive chair—when you're comfortable, you'll be able to work for longer periods of time, and you'll find the overall experience more pleasant. When you set up your studio, keep all your materials within easy reach, and make sure you have adequate artificial light if you work at night. It is also helpful to sort your pastels by color and value (see page 6) to make it easier to find the colors you want while you are painting.

SUPPLIES **Since 1766, Reeves has been manufacturing excellent quality paints and brushes and has long been established around the world as a wonderful source of art material for beginners. Reeves products are available at art supply stores everywhere.**

Problem

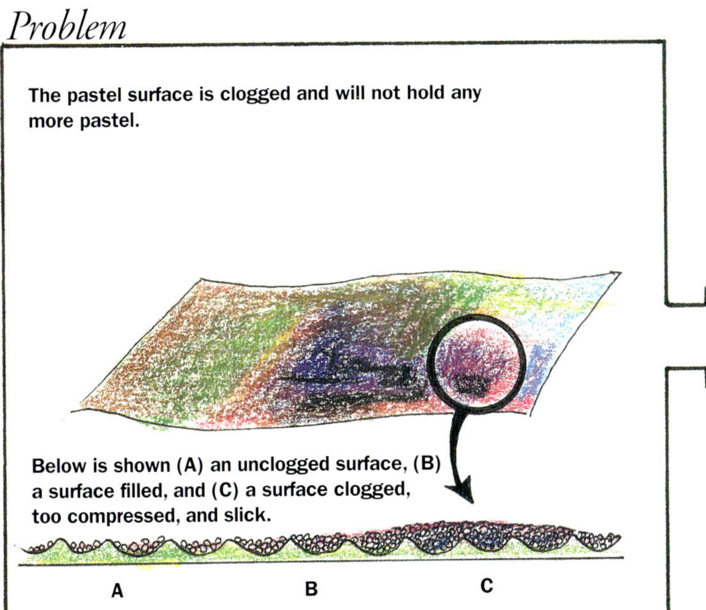

The pastel surface is clogged and will not hold any more pastel.

Below is shown (A) an unclogged surface, (B) a surface filled, and (C) a surface clogged, too compressed, and slick.

Solutions

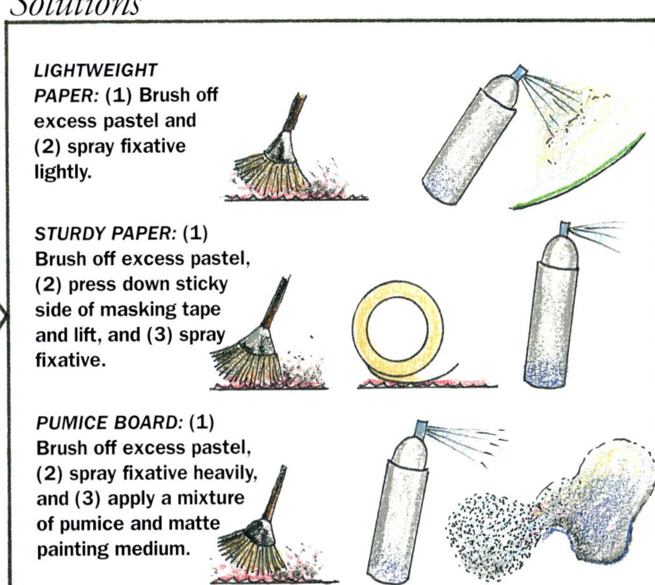

LIGHTWEIGHT PAPER: (1) Brush off excess pastel and (2) spray fixative lightly.

STURDY PAPER: (1) Brush off excess pastel, (2) press down sticky side of masking tape and lift, and (3) spray fixative.

PUMICE BOARD: (1) Brush off excess pastel, (2) spray fixative heavily, and (3) apply a mixture of pumice and matte painting medium.

Problems

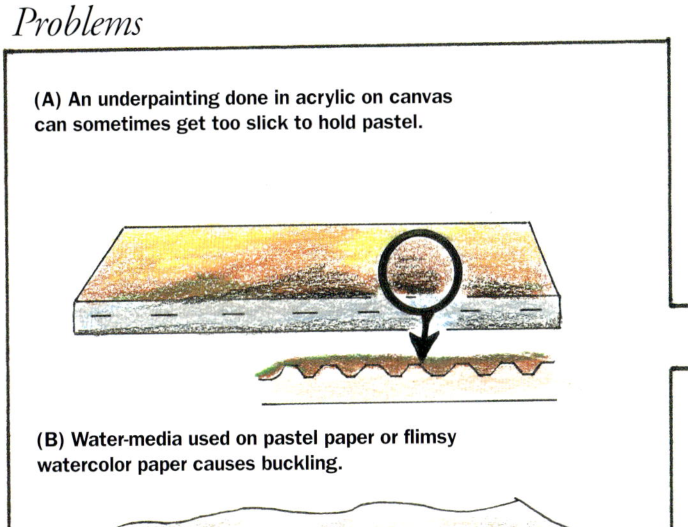

(A) An underpainting done in acrylic on canvas can sometimes get too slick to hold pastel.

(B) Water-media used on pastel paper or flimsy watercolor paper causes buckling.

Solutions

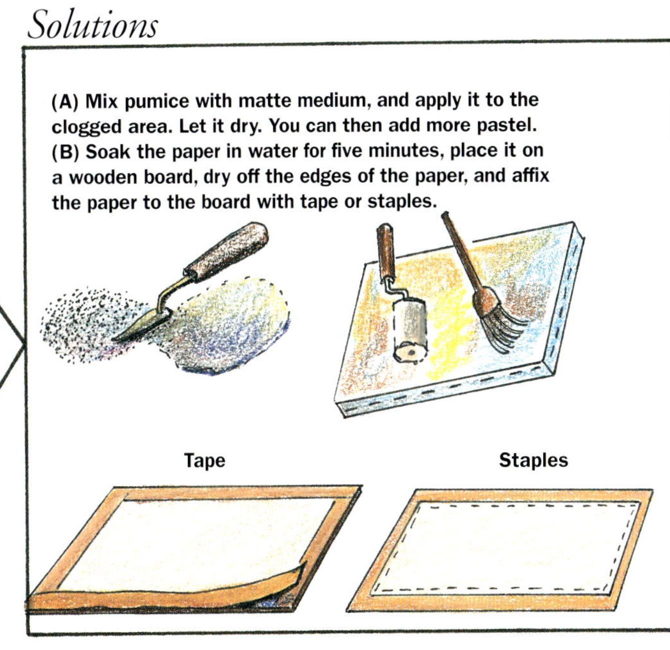

(A) Mix pumice with matte medium, and apply it to the clogged area. Let it dry. You can then add more pastel.
(B) Soak the paper in water for five minutes, place it on a wooden board, dry off the edges of the paper, and affix the paper to the board with tape or staples.

Problems

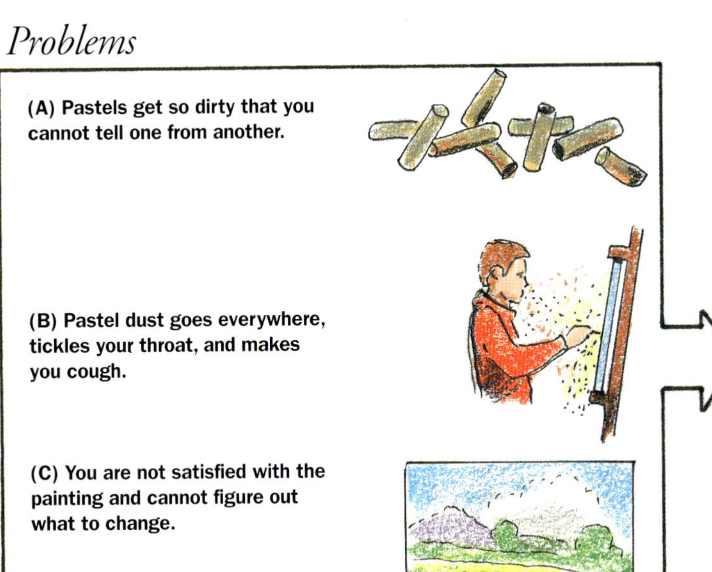

(A) Pastels get so dirty that you cannot tell one from another.

(B) Pastel dust goes everywhere, tickles your throat, and makes you cough.

(C) You are not satisfied with the painting and cannot figure out what to change.

Solutions

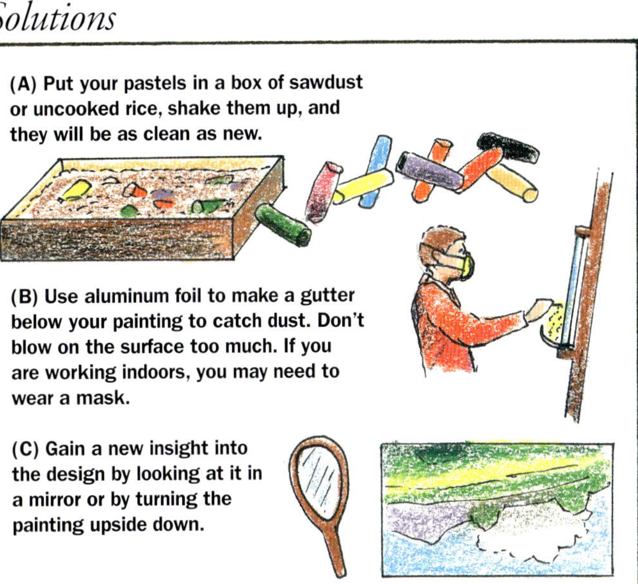

(A) Put your pastels in a box of sawdust or uncooked rice, shake them up, and they will be as clean as new.

(B) Use aluminum foil to make a gutter below your painting to catch dust. Don't blow on the surface too much. If you are working indoors, you may need to wear a mask.

(C) Gain a new insight into the design by looking at it in a mirror or by turning the painting upside down.

Color Theory

Knowing a little about basic color theory can help you tremendously in painting with pastels. There are three *primary* colors (yellow, red, and blue); all other colors are derived from these three. *Secondary* colors (purple, green, and orange) are a combination of two primaries (for example, mixing red and blue makes purple). *Tertiary* colors are those that you get when you mix a primary with a secondary color (such as red orange, red purple, or blue-green). And the term *complementary* refers to colors that are directly across from each other on the color wheel. In addition, there are other terms to remember when mixing colors: *Hue* refers to the color itself (such as blue or purple), *intensity* means the strength or *chroma* of a color (in pastel, usually gauged by pressure applied), and *value* is the lightness or darkness of color. For more information on color properties and values, see the examples below.

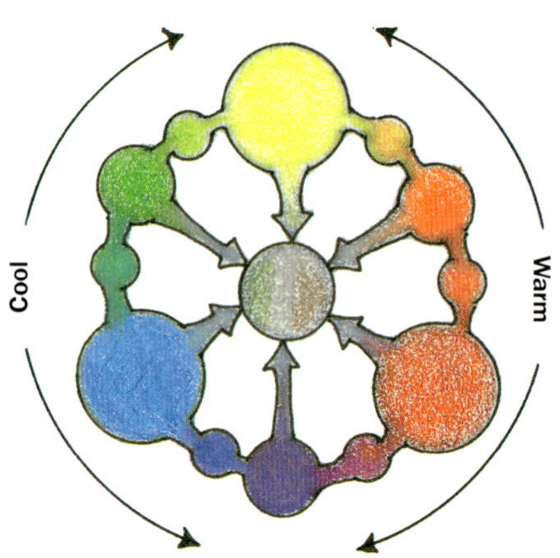

PROPERTIES OF COLOR **In the standard color wheel shown above, you can see four properties of color: (1) value (colors drop in value from yellow toward violet); (2) hue; (3) chroma (colors become grayer toward the center); and (4) temperature (warm versus cool colors). The so-called warm colors are the reds, oranges, and yellows, and the cool colors are the blues, greens, and purples.**

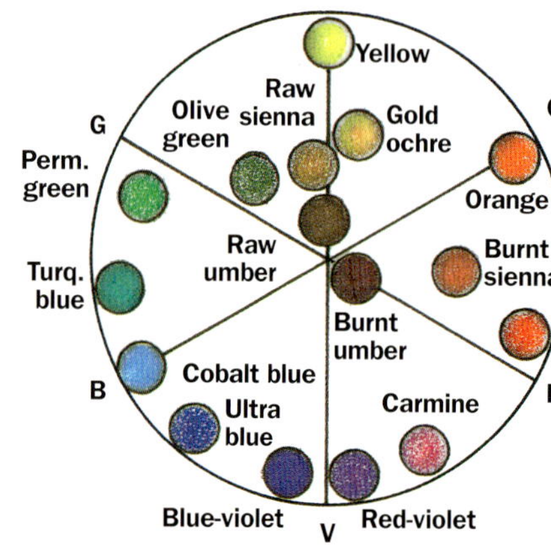

CHROMA OF COLOR **The diagram above shows the position of various pastel colors on the color wheel in relation to their chroma: The farther from the center of the wheel the color is, the higher its chroma. For example, raw umber is a low chroma yellow, and burnt sienna is a low chroma red-orange. Permanent red and turquoise have more intensity, so they sit farther from the center.**

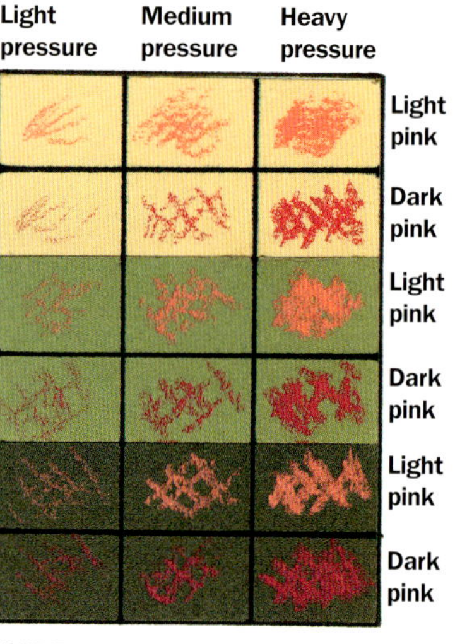

PRESSURE AND VALUES **On toned (colored) paper, pressure is a key element in determining values. Here you can see how two values of the same color appear when applied with different amounts of pressure. From left to right above, light, medium, and heavy strokes from only one light or dark pastel yield at least three values. (See page 11 for more on how using toned paper can affect your work.)**

Surface Mixing Pastel Colors

SMOOTH BLEND **Here side strokes of yellow are layered smoothly over blue to create a bright green, which has more life and interest than a manufactured green.**

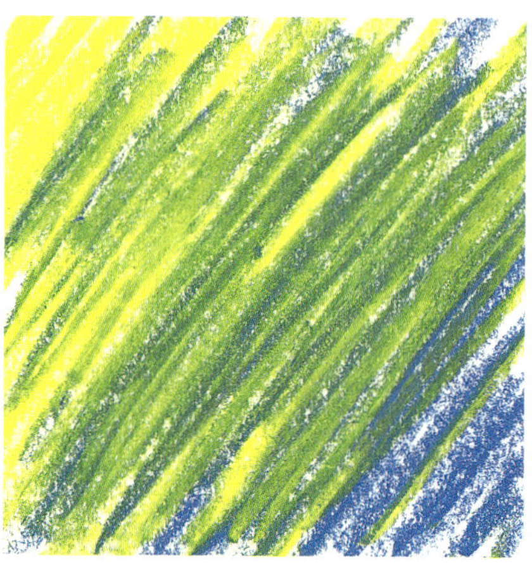

UNBLENDED STROKES **Choppy, unblended strokes of yellow and blue create the impression of green. Instead of blending the colors on the paper, the eye visually mixes them.**

MIXING THREE COLORS **Here strokes of lavender and turquoise are layered over blue. This creates a richer color than a mix of just two colors does.**

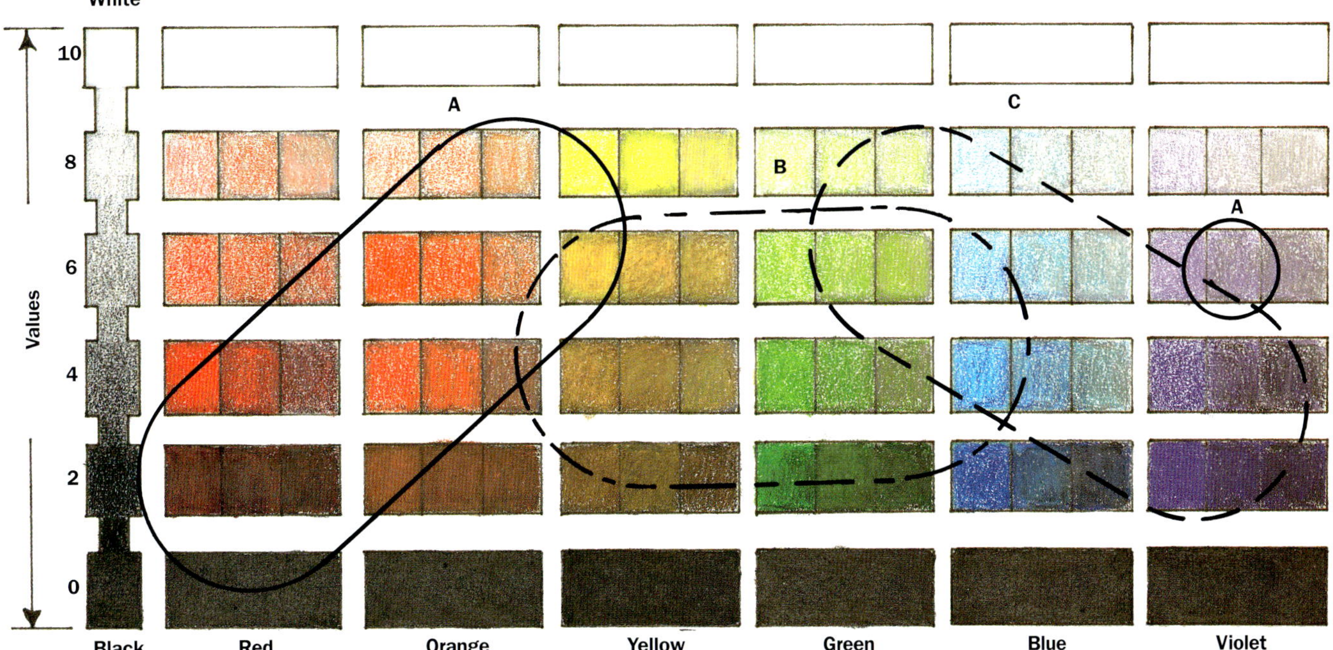

CHARTING VALUES **Although the value scale on this chart goes from 0 (black) to 10 (white), most pastel sets have only three or four values; this is not usually a problem, since you can create your own mixtures by adding black or white to the pure color.**

Choosing a Range of Values

The color chart above approximates the range of pastel colors you should have in your set. For example, when you reach for a red (column 1), you should be able to locate at least three values of red: a light *tint* (the color plus white), a pure hue, and a dark *shade* (the color plus black). These colors correspond to the gray scale at the left of the color chart. In addition, you should have several intensities of red. The red in each row in the chart gets a little grayer from left to right—these are your "earth colors." This chart is also helpful for visualizing various color schemes, such as single-color, or *monochromatic* schemes (all colors in one column); similar, or *analogous* harmonies (neighboring columns combined), or complementary harmonies (skip two columns; for example, red and green). Ovals A, B, and C show how three different analogous color schemes were applied to the three sketches of the same view shown at right. (For more on color in pastel, see *Portraits* by Ken Goldman in the pastel section of Walter Foster's How to Draw and Paint series.)

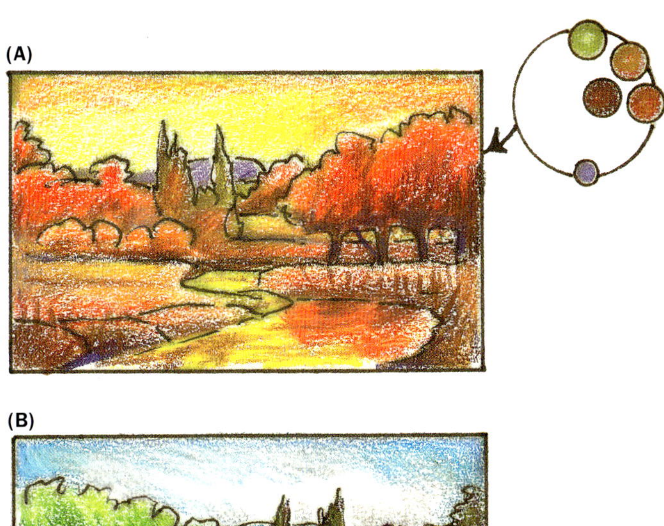

Using Analogous Colors

Analogous colors are those that are adjacent to each other on the color wheel, such as yellow, reddish yellow, and yellowish red. Example A to the right shows a warm analogous color harmony with an accent of violet (autumn colors). Example B is an analogous scheme with more natural colors and burnt sienna accents (a summer scene). And example C shows color harmonies like those at dawn or dusk. Experiment with different color harmonies and try some additional studies of your own.

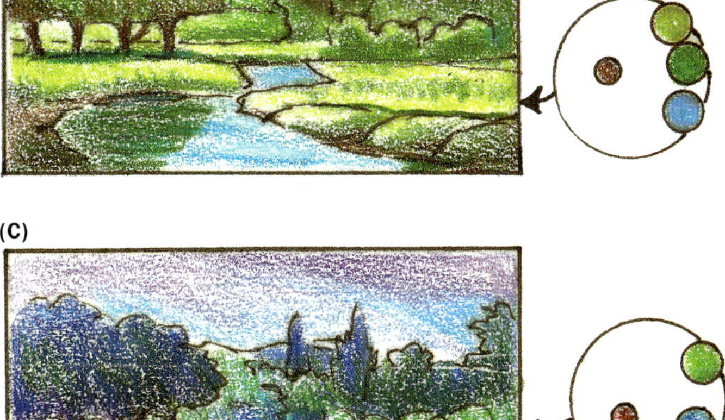

Soft Pastel Techniques

Grips

Working with soft pastels allows you to apply color directly to the support, without any type of tool or brush to "translate" your strokes. This means that the way you hold the pastel stick (overhand or underhand), where you hold it, and the amount of pressure you apply will affect the stroke you create. Although there is no "correct" way to hold your pastels, it's a good idea to experiment with different grips to learn what types of strokes each one will help you produce.

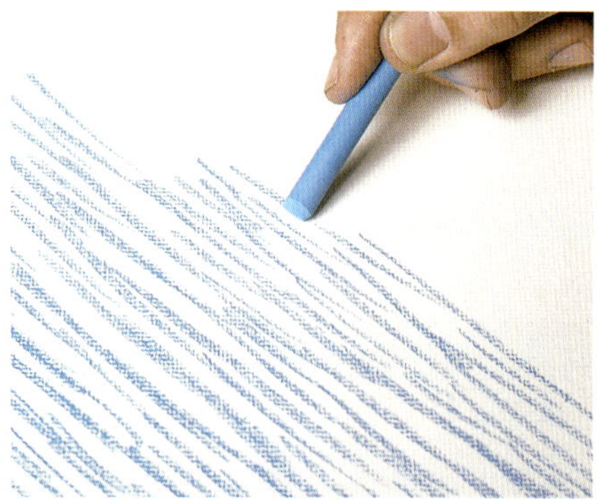

USING THE POINT **Grip the pastel stick near the back end and use the point (or the edge of the flat tip) to create thin, fairly even lines for linear textures, such as long grasses or wood grain.**

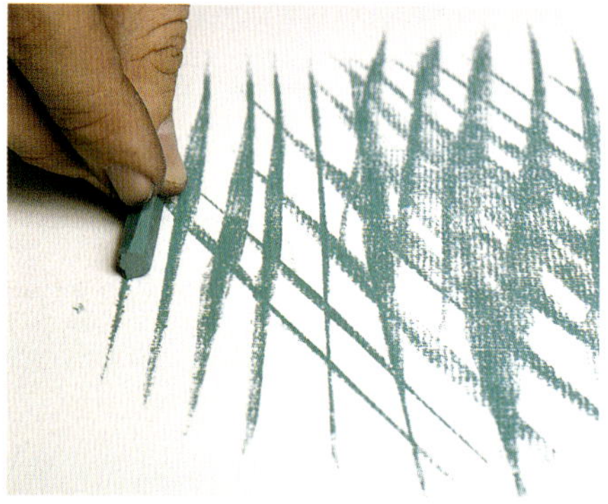

USING THE SIDE **Place the stick on the support, press down on its length, and stroke either lengthwise or sideways to create thick, overlapping, haphazard lines, as for background textures.**

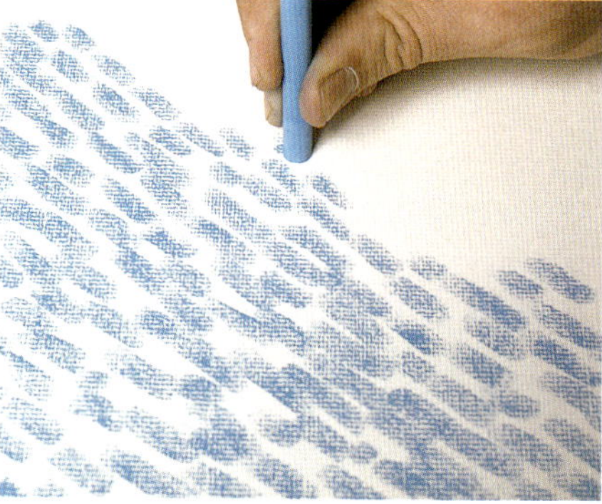

USING THE END **Hold the pastel stick vertically on the support, and grip it near the tip. Then use the end to make thick, rounded strokes for elements such as cobbled roads or brickwork.**

Masking

When working with soft pastel, the dusty nature of the medium sometimes makes it difficult to create clean, hard edges. One solution to this dilemma is to use a masking technique to create sharp edges. If you need a straight line, you can use the edge of a clean piece of paper as a guide. Just lay it over your support, secure it in place with artist's tape, and apply the pastel over the edge. When you're done painting, carefully peel the top sheet away to avoid smudging. For a clean-edged shape, you can create a special mask with tracing paper in any shape you like, as shown below.

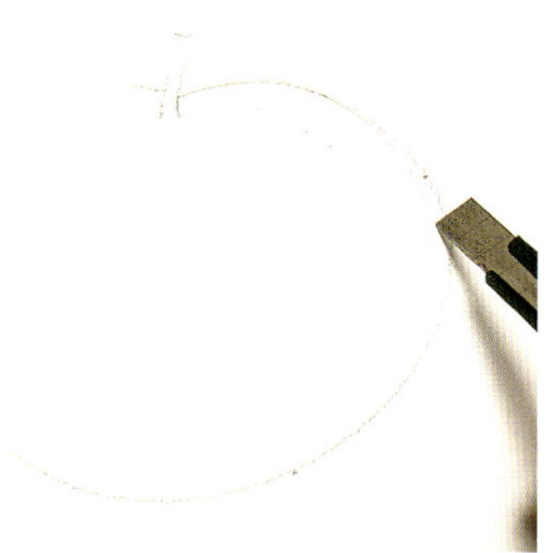

CUT THE SHAPE **Begin by drawing the shape on a piece of tracing paper and cutting it out.**

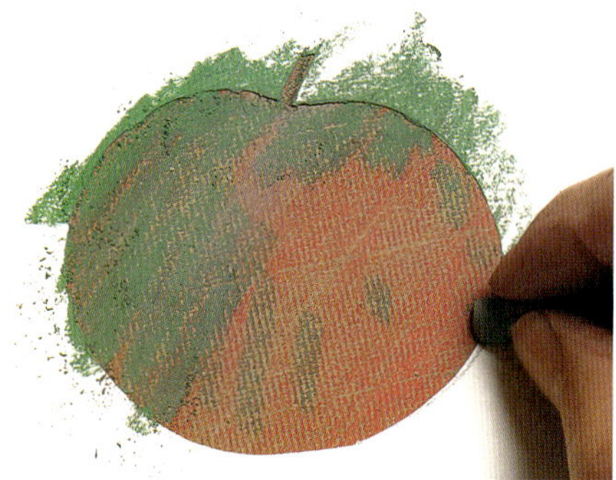

APPLY THE COLOR **After painting the background, apply the mask and then add color.**

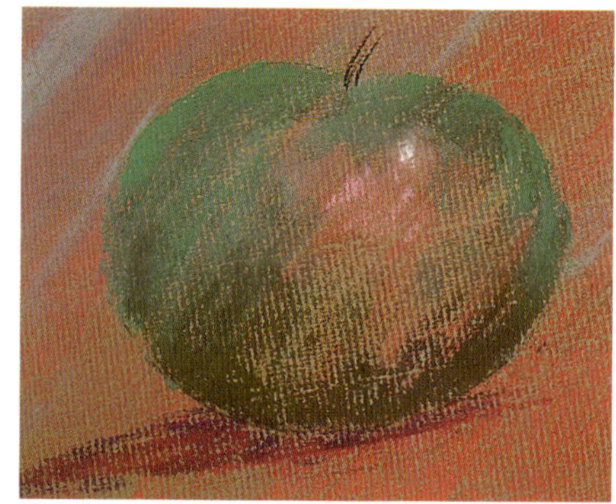

REMOVE THE MASK **Carefully peel away the mask to reveal the crisp shape underneath.**

Strokes

Pastel can be applied with sharp, linear marks or soft, broad strokes of color and texture, depending on the effect you wish to create. Here are some examples of strokes you can practice as you explore the possibilities of working with pastel.

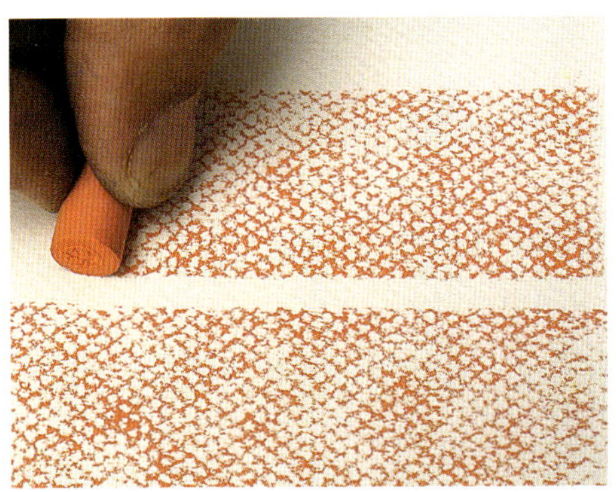

SIDE STROKES **Use the entire length of the pastel stick to quickly fill in areas of broad color, as for skies and water.**

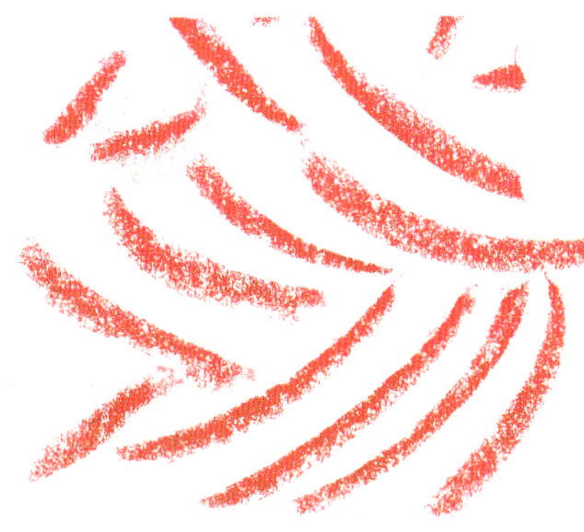

FIRM STROKES **Use heavy pressure and the tip of the pastel to create thick, bold strokes for linear elements, such as stems and branches.**

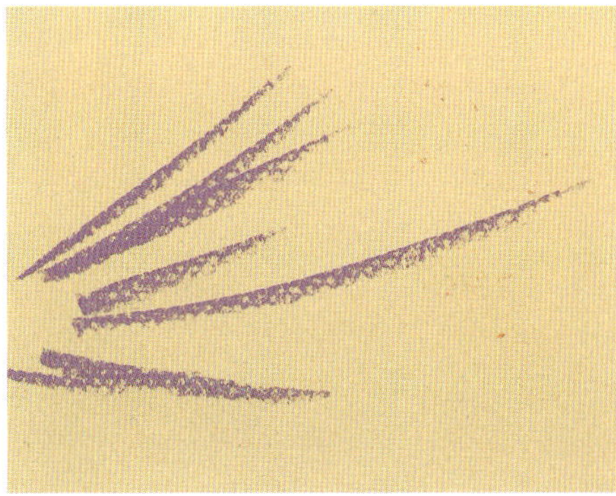

TAPERED STROKES **Apply more pressure at the bottom of the stroke and lighten the pressure as you end the stroke for animal hair or feathers.**

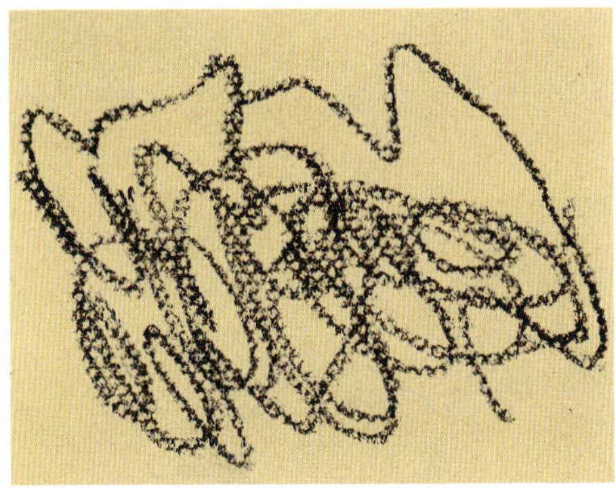

RANDOM STROKES **Use random, scribbling strokes to convey texture (like that of distant foliage) or to create shading. Hold the pastel stick lightly and keep your wrist loose.**

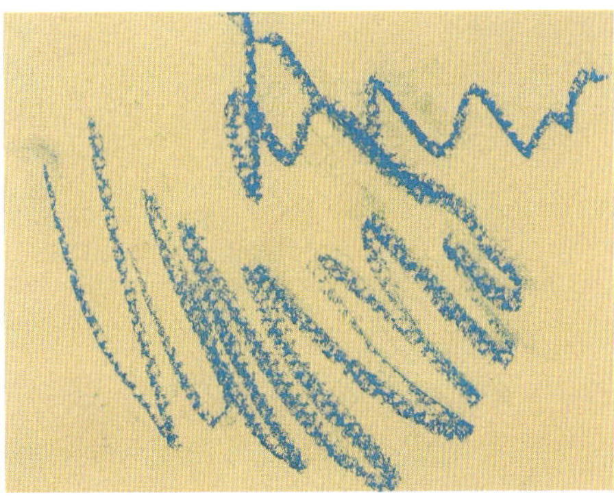

SQUIGGLY LINES **Create free-form, squiggly lines with the end of a large pastel stick to help convey the look of waves or the movement of running water.**

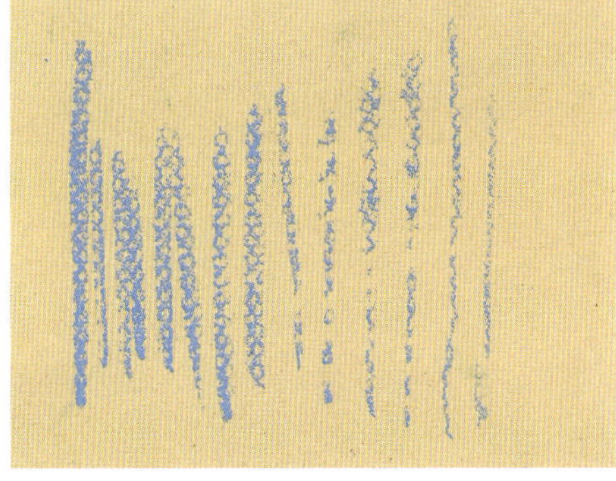

VARYING PRESSURE **Use heavier pressure (at left) to make thick, dark lines for reflections in still water, and use lighter pressure (at right) to create thinner, broken strokes for ripples.**

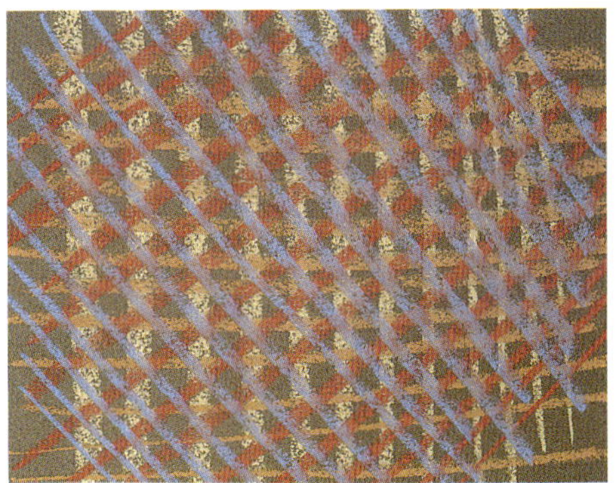

CROSS-HATCHING **Lay one set of lines over another (in a different direction) to imitate a pattern, depict texture in cloth, or cover a large area without oversaturating the support.**

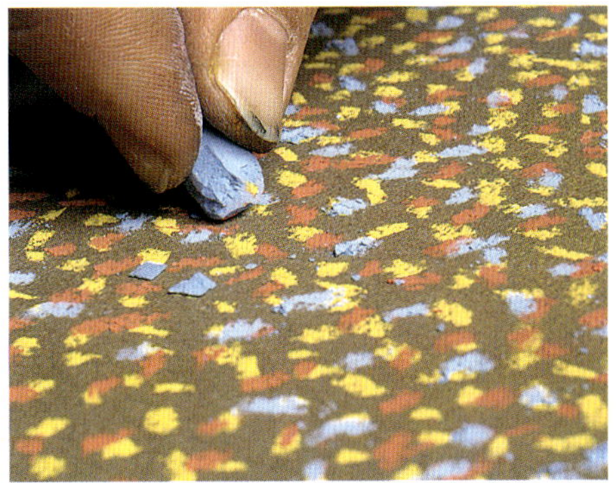

POINTILLISM **Use a series of dots to build color for backgrounds or other large areas of color. Viewed from a distance, the dots appear to merge into one color, as the eye visually blends them.**

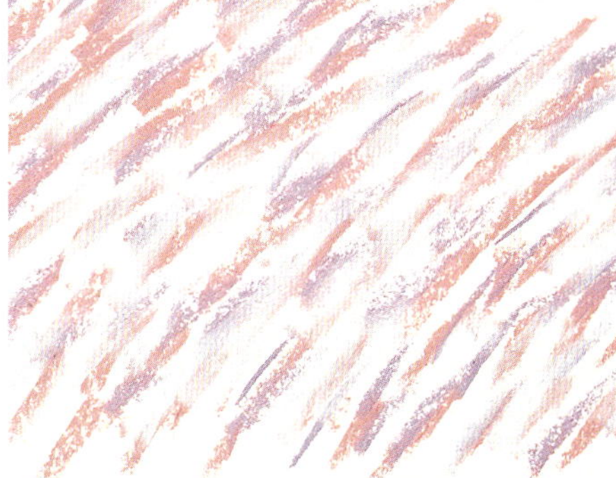

FEATHERING **Layer feathery, light, diagonal strokes of various colors to create the rough textures of stucco or rock, an uneven ground, or a swift-moving river.**

Blending

Learning how to blend and layer soft pastels is essential because, unlike other painting media, the colors are not premixed on a palette. You must apply the hues directly to the support and mix them there. You can blend the strokes thoroughly to create a solid area of smooth color, or you can leave visible strokes of various hues if you want more texture. You can also use your fingers, the side of your hand, or any number of blending tools to achieve a variety of blends, ranging from rough to smooth.

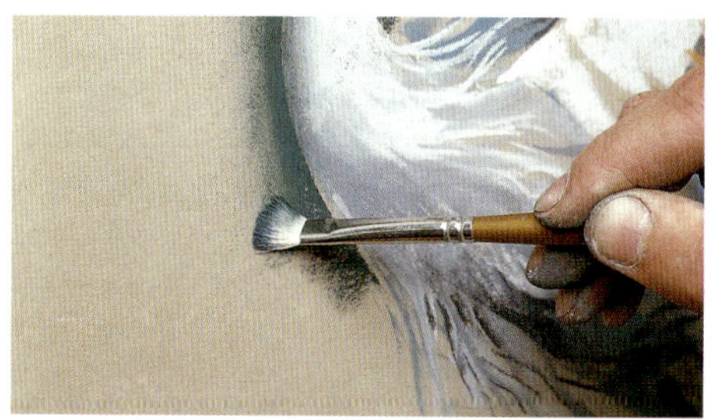

BLENDING WITH A BRUSH **You can use a bristle brush (either synthetic or natural hair) to break up the pastel particles and spread the color evenly on the support, as shown above.**

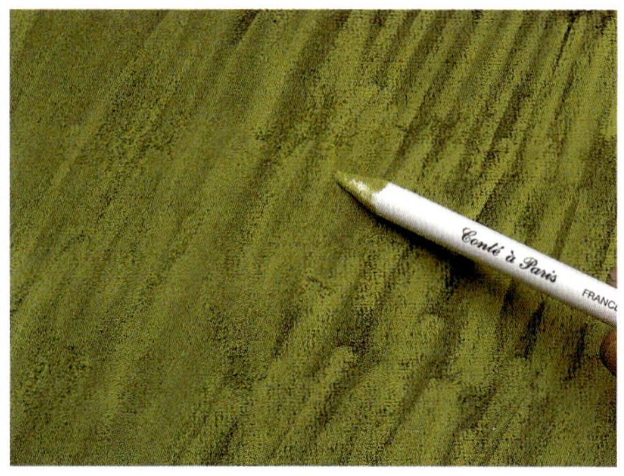

BLENDING WITH A TORTILLON **For soft blends, gently rub a paper blending stump (also called a "tortillon" or "torchon") over the pigment.**

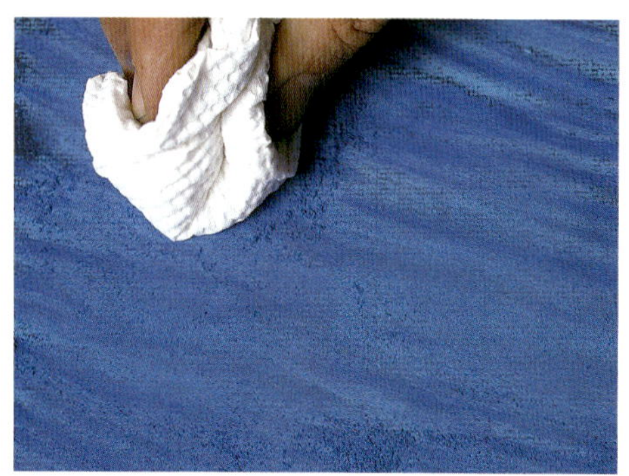

BLENDING WITH A RAG **Use a soft, lint-free paper towel or rag to blend large areas of color. Take care not to wipe off too much of the pigment.**

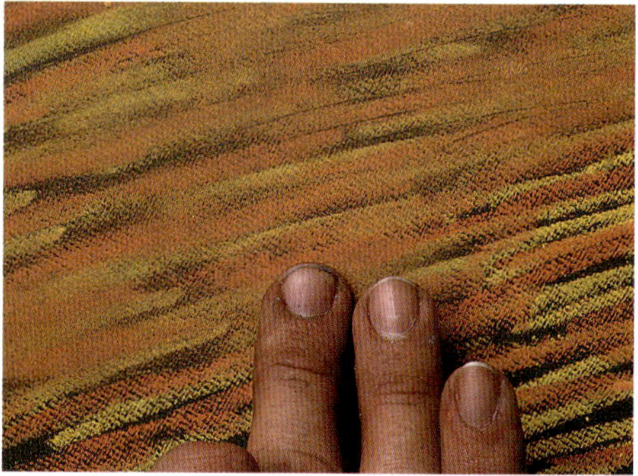

BLENDING WITH YOUR HAND **Use your fingers or the side or your hand to work the pastel deeply into the tooth of the paper.**

Correcting Mistakes

There are a number of techniques you can try to correct any pastel mishaps. If the pigment hasn't been applied too heavily, use a kneaded eraser to lift off some color. (Just take care that you don't rub the particles deeper into the support.) You can also use the tip of a craft knife to gently scrape off pigment, but you must be very careful not to damage the surface of the paper underneath. Another approach is to use a combination of techniques, as shown here.

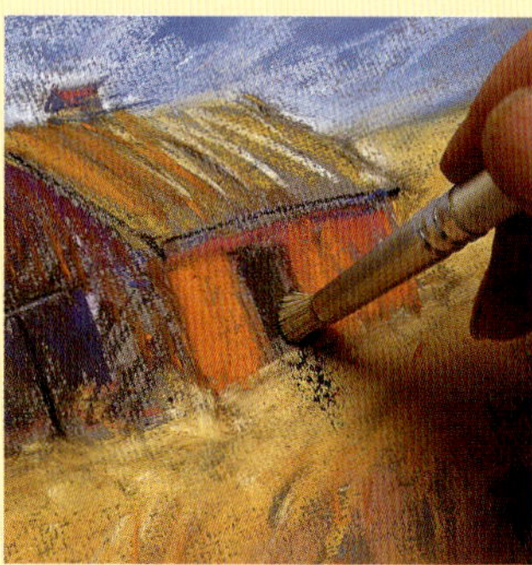

REMOVE COLOR **First use a stiff bristle brush to brush off the color you wish to correct.**

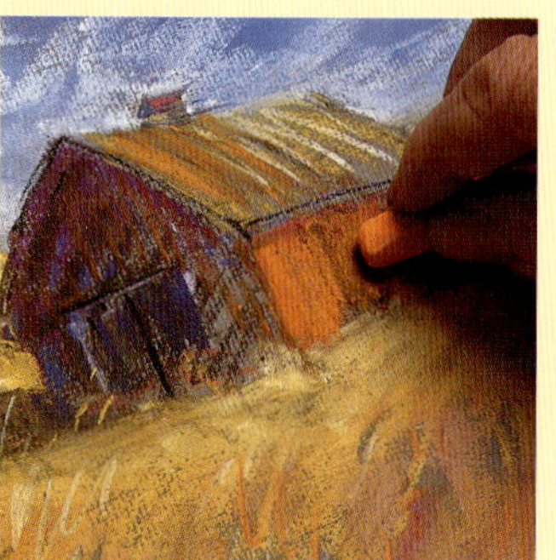

REAPPLY COLOR **Then reapply the pigment to the area using a different hue.**

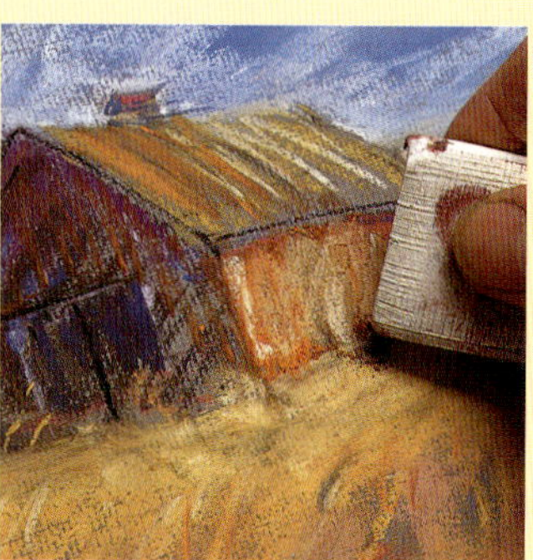

LIFT OFF THE REMAINDERS **Use a kneaded eraser to pick up and lift off any stray particles.**

Using Colored Paper

Pastel papers come in a variety of colors; if you choose a colored paper that shares a dominant hue in your painting, you can create harmony among the colors in your painting and save a significant amount of time, as the colored paper provides a medium value on which to build color. Notice how the colors of the papers below affect the same image in different ways.

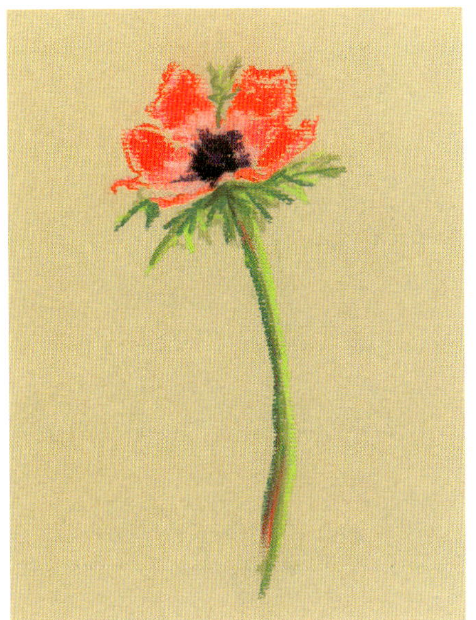

BEIGE PAPER On the beige paper, the dark center has a greater visual impact.

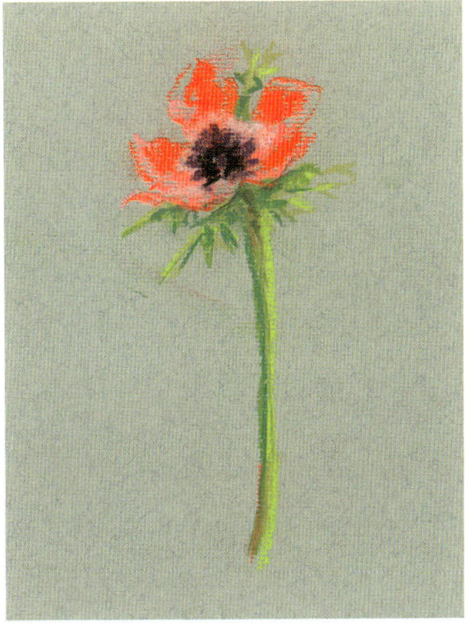

GRAY PAPER On the gray paper, the green stem has less strength.

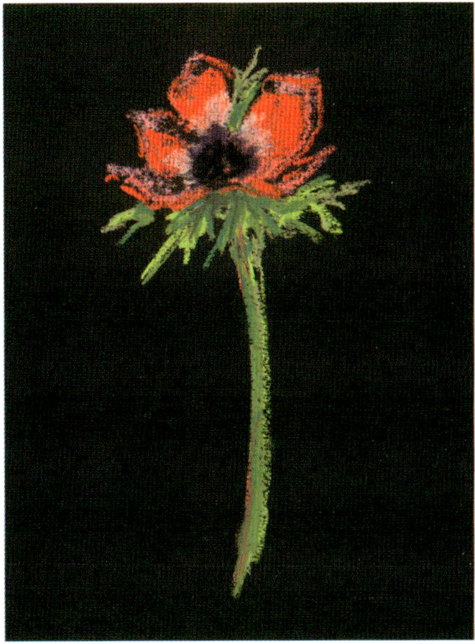

BLACK PAPER The contrasts are the most dramatic on the black paper.

Using Fixative

Many artists use some type of spray-on sealer or fixative to set their work and prevent smearing. Some artists fix their paintings as they go, beginning with a thick layer of initial color. Then they spray the first layer with sealer, which can be painted over with subsequent layers without the risk of smudging. Varnish, however, may darken and thicken the pigment. An alternative is to lay a piece of tissue paper over your painting and cover it with a board. Then apply firm, even pressure to push the pastel particles farther into the surface of the paper so they adhere better.

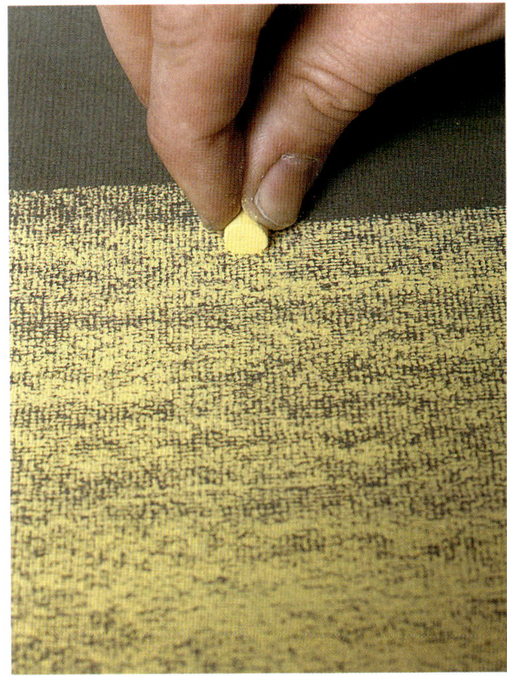

FIXING STAGE ONE **To decide whether the fixative you have will adversely affect the colors, make a practice test by laying down a thick layer of pigment on a piece of pastel paper.**

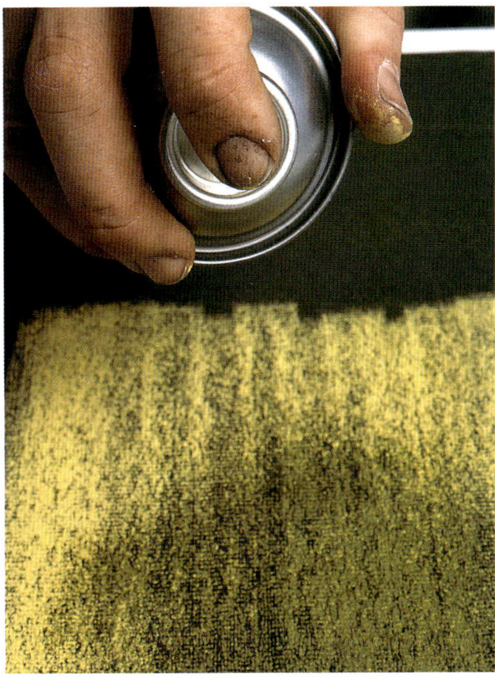

FIXING STAGE TWO **Spray the piece with an even layer of fixative. If the color stays true, you can varnish your work as you go, painting over each fixed layer without the risk of smudging.**

Lesson One: Flowers

Flowers are wonderful subjects for pastel paintings. They are not only easily accessible, but they are also incredibly diverse. In fact, there are so many different types of flowers that you can produce dozens of paintings without ever portraying the same flower twice. And although you can always paint just a single blossom, a bouquet of several flowers offers the opportunity to use the brilliant pigments of pastel to their fullest. But choosing what flowers to include is just the first step; the next is to decide how to place them. When arranging a group of flowers, strive for a composition that creates a sense of movement. Fight the tendency to make all the flowers the same size, to space them regularly, and to place them in even rows. Your painting will be more interesting and effective if the arrangement is asymmetrical and the blossoms aren't all carbon copies of one another.

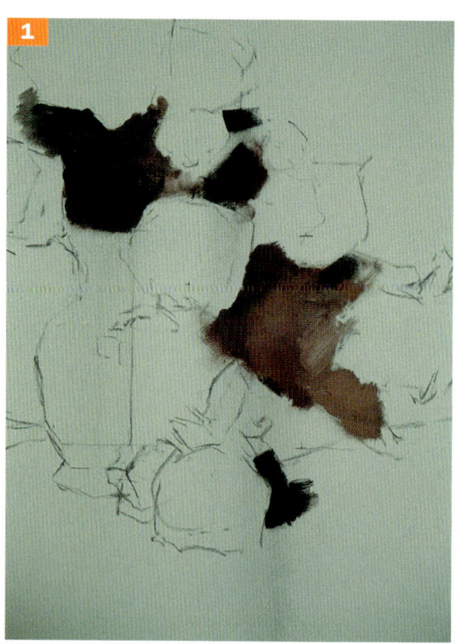

STEP ONE Draw the main shapes using vine charcoal on a dark-toned, sanded pastel board. Place the center of interest (the second peony from the left) slightly off-center, and position another blossom in front of the vase to draw in the viewer's eye. Then paint the darkest areas, using dark values of ivory black and carmine brown, working the colors into the support with a brush dampened in denatured alcohol.

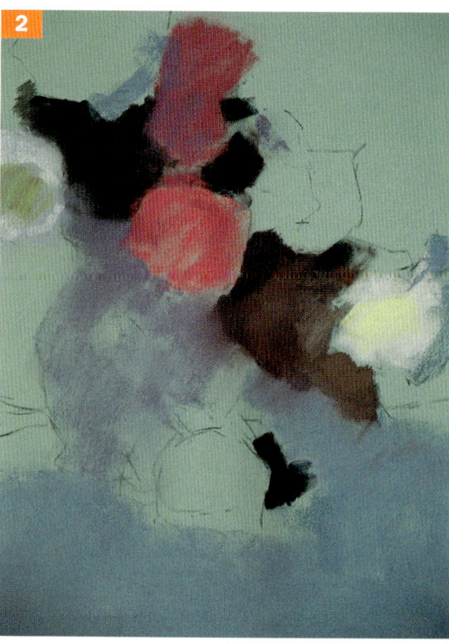

STEP TWO Next use light blue-gray and light lemon yellow to establish the lightest value: the flower on the right. Then apply madder lake deep—the most intense color—for the flower that's the center of interest. Next paint in the background flowers with Indian red and dark blue-gray, and block in the tabletop with mouse gray. Use dark blue-violet for the vase, and blend the strokes with a paper stump.

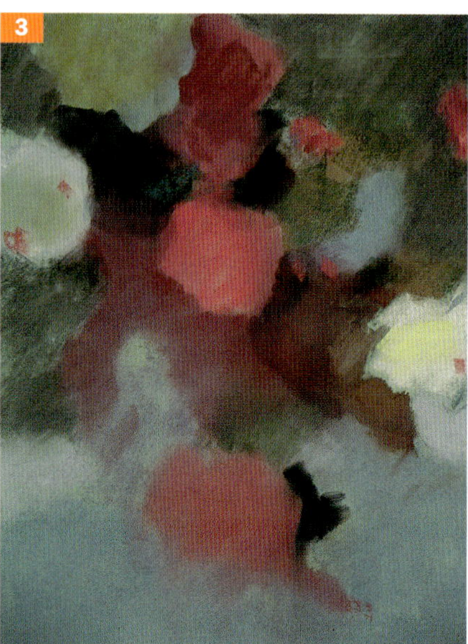

STEP THREE Fill in the background with dark gray-green, and create some leaves in dark olive green. Create the flowers on the table with madder lake deep and the bud on the right with Indian red. Then add dark Indian red to the vase and blue-gray to the middle white flower.

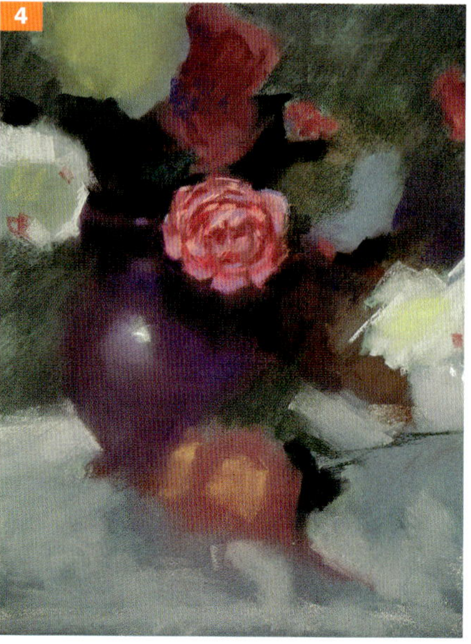

STEP FOUR Add the main flower with dark cobalt violet, blue-violet, carmine, light permanent rose, and dark burgundy. Draw the peony stems with dark blue-green and yellow. Then define the vase with dark cobalt violet, black, blue-violet, and a stroke of light phthalo green.

STEP FIVE Now add blue-gray to the white flower on the lower right. Paint the dark recesses between the petals with dark blue-violet, olive green, and dark yellow ochre. For the pink flowers, use Indian red, light red-violet, and lemon yellow; the leaves are olive green.

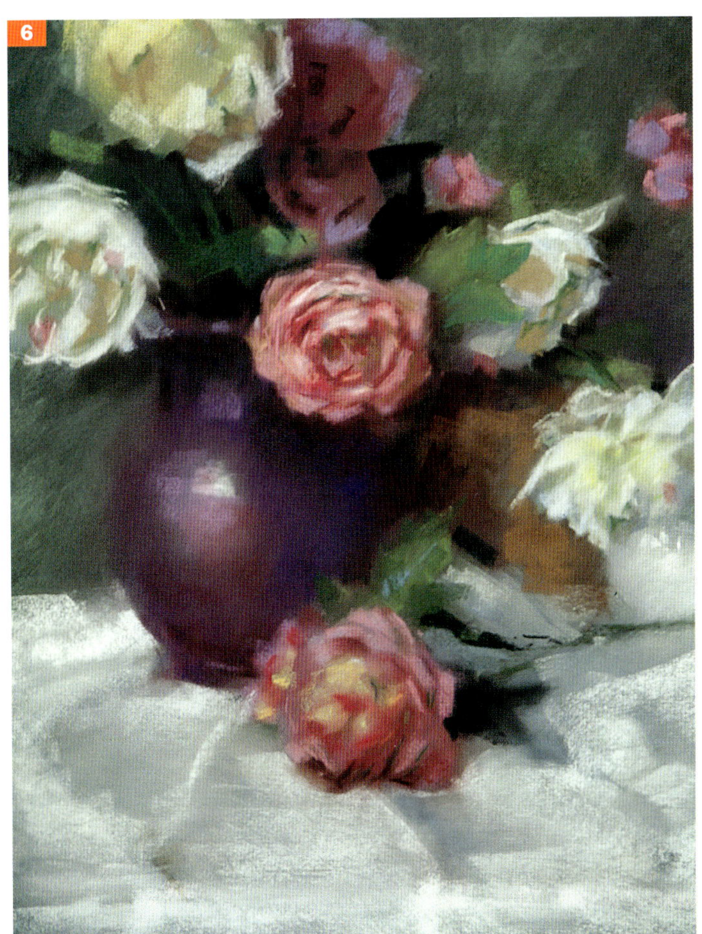

STEP SIX Add blue-violet for the lights on the distant pink flower and buds. Refine the light peony at the top left with simple strokes of blue-gray, and indicate the recesses with dark yellow ochre. As you move away from the center of interest, paint less detail. In fact, that's exactly how you see. When you look right at something, you see sharp edges and a wealth of detail; but objects in your peripheral vision appear less crisp and defined. (Of course, if you turn your gaze to them, then they become clearer.)

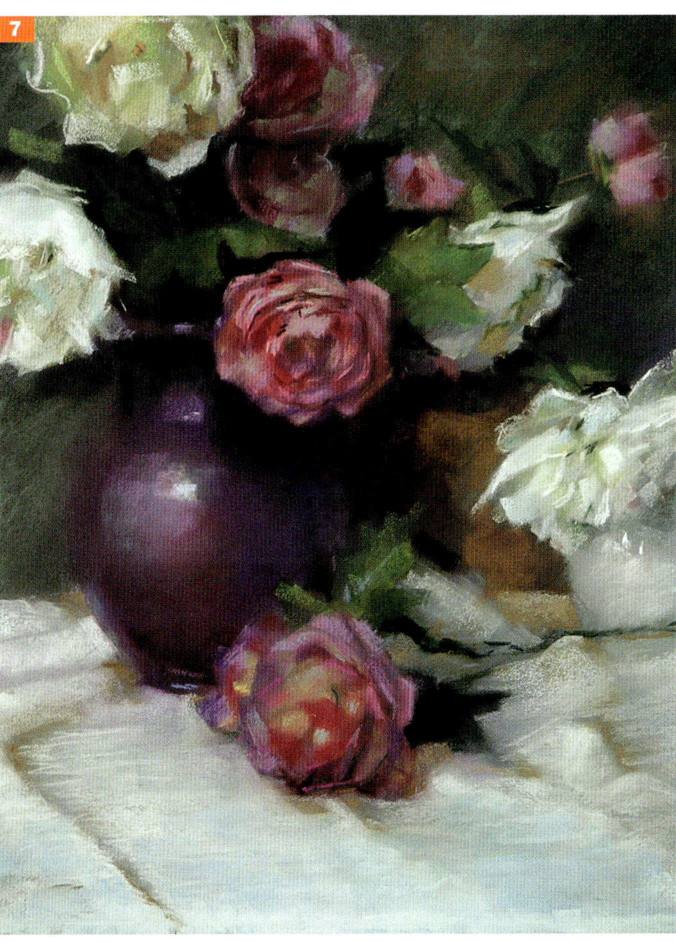

STEP SEVEN Darken the center of interest with permanent rose and blue-violet, and refine the petals' outlines to make them less regular. Then darken the vase with dark cobalt violet, and simplify the folds in the tablecloth with light blue-gray. Use a very light value of phthalocyanine *(phthalo)* blue to make the light at the edge of the table appear to come forward, and define the outer petals of the three top white peonies with light blue-gray. Finally add a few small, sharp strokes of light cobalt blue for the highlights on the vase.

Understanding Pastel Numbering Systems

Pastel manufacturers produce each hue in a variety of full-strength colors and in a wide range of dark and light values (made by adding black or white; see pages 6 and 7). And many manufacturers label their pastels using a numbering system to identify the strength of each color. Unfortunately these numbering systems are not standardized among brands. For example, one manufacturer labels the pure color as 5, with the lightest value being a 1 and the darkest a 9. Another brand uses decimal points to denote the proportion of white that has been added to each pure hue. When you purchase pastels, note whether a numbering system is used. If so, make a chart for future reference; color a patch on your chart, and write down its name and number so you will know what to buy when restocking your supply.

Lesson Two: Plein Air Pastel

The best thing you can do to hone your artistic skills is to go outdoors and paint directly from life. And because pastel is such a rapid and responsive medium, it is ideal for painting *en plein air* and recording the effects that can change so quickly in nature. Morning dew, shifting clouds, crashing waves—all can be captured with a few quick, decisive strokes. Another advantage of pastel is that you don't have to premix any pigments, wait for the colors to dry, or worry about keeping brushes clean—in short, there are no tiresome procedures to dampen your spirits or lessen your response to the subject. And because you don't need the extra supplies that some other media require—such as brushes, knives, or mixing mediums—your traveling art pack can be light and easy to carry. Then just lay out your pastels, and you're ready to start!

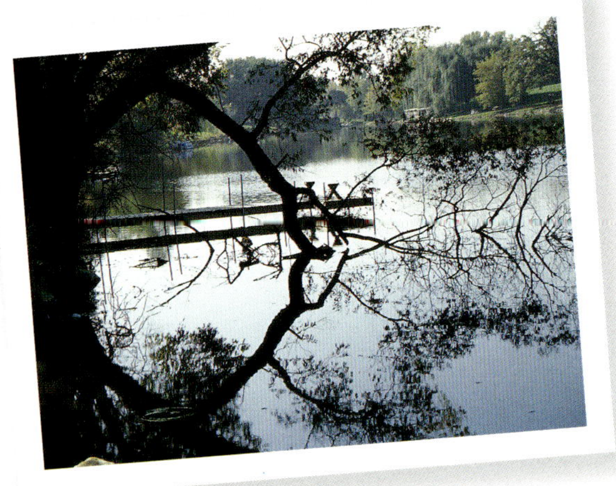

WORKING FROM LIFE Even though it may seem more convenient to paint from photos, they're really only pale imitations of nature. Compare this photo to the final painting, and notice the nuances of color and value that are lost in the photograph. The two darkest values both become black, and the lightest values turn to white.

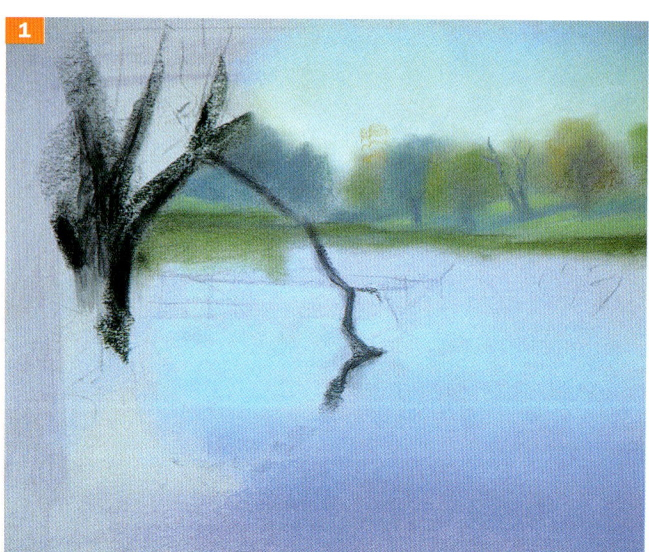

STEP ONE Begin by toning the light areas of a light blue paper with thin layers of light yellow, light red-violet, and cobalt blue, using the side of your hand to rub the pastel into the tooth of the paper. Then sketch in the scene with vine charcoal, and apply black to the tree mass. Paint the sky with layers of cobalt blue near the top, light turquoise and light raw sienna in the middle, and light cobalt blue near the bottom. Next paint the trees on the far shore with mouse gray for the trunks and deepest shadows and olive green for the light areas. Gray the trees with a layer of red-violet to enhance the sense of depth. Then add blue-green to a few trees and burnt sienna to another, blending each stroke with the side of your finger.

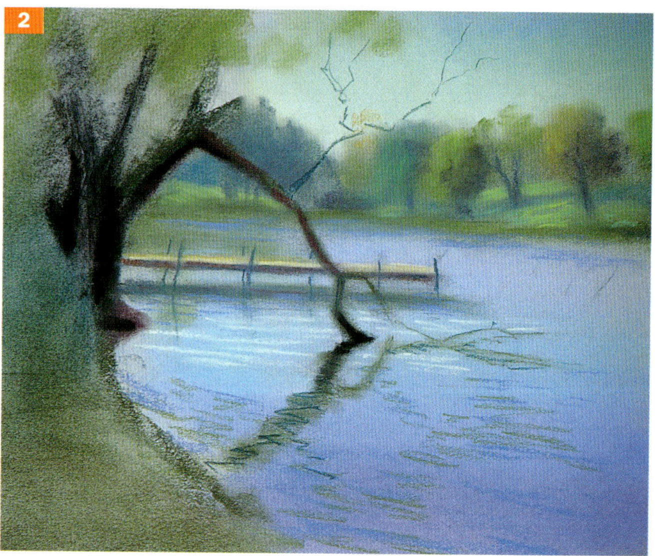

STEP TWO Add blue-violet and cobalt blue to the foreground water and light red-violet to the background. Then blend the color transitions in the sky and water with the side of your hand, and add a few strokes of light lemon yellow for the highlights on the water. For the pale areas of the dock, use light gold ochre; for the darks, use mouse gray and dark red-violet deep. Block in the general mass of the closest tree using dark olive green. Then start to add a warm dark Indian red to the trunk. Paint deep reflections on the water with dark olive green and dark gray-green, and work light chrome green grayed with light red-violet to areas on the far shore to indicate the sunlit grass.

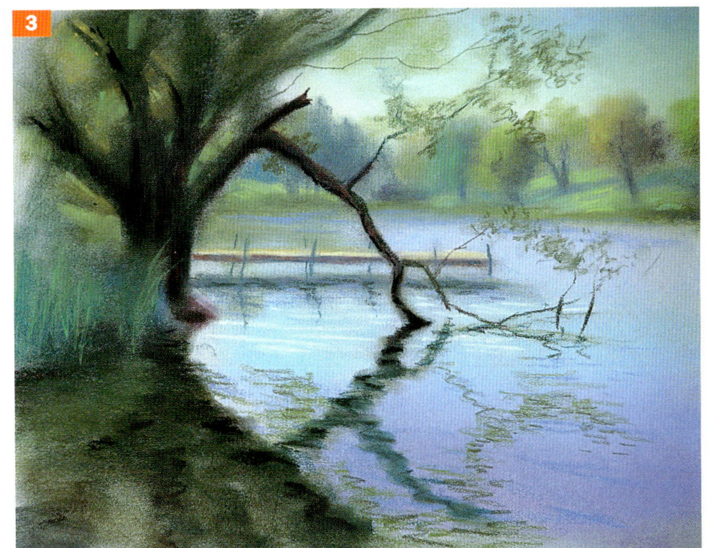

STEP THREE Concentrate on darkening the tree mass with dark gray-green and dark burnt sienna, and use the same colors to deepen the reflections in the water. Sharpen the edges of the broken branch by painting some of the sky color into it. Next add leaves with dark olive green, and define the spaces between the branches (the *negative spaces*) with strokes of light olive green and orange. Then use a few strokes of olive green to indicate the grass near the tree trunk. Use ultramarine blue to represent the "sky holes" in the reflection of the tree, and blend your strokes less so that they appear bolder. Use cobalt blue to indicate ripples cutting across the reflected branches. Then add a few more warm shadows to the trees with dark burnt sienna. Next add a hint of the sky color behind the tree with cobalt blue, and blend it into some of the spaces between branches.

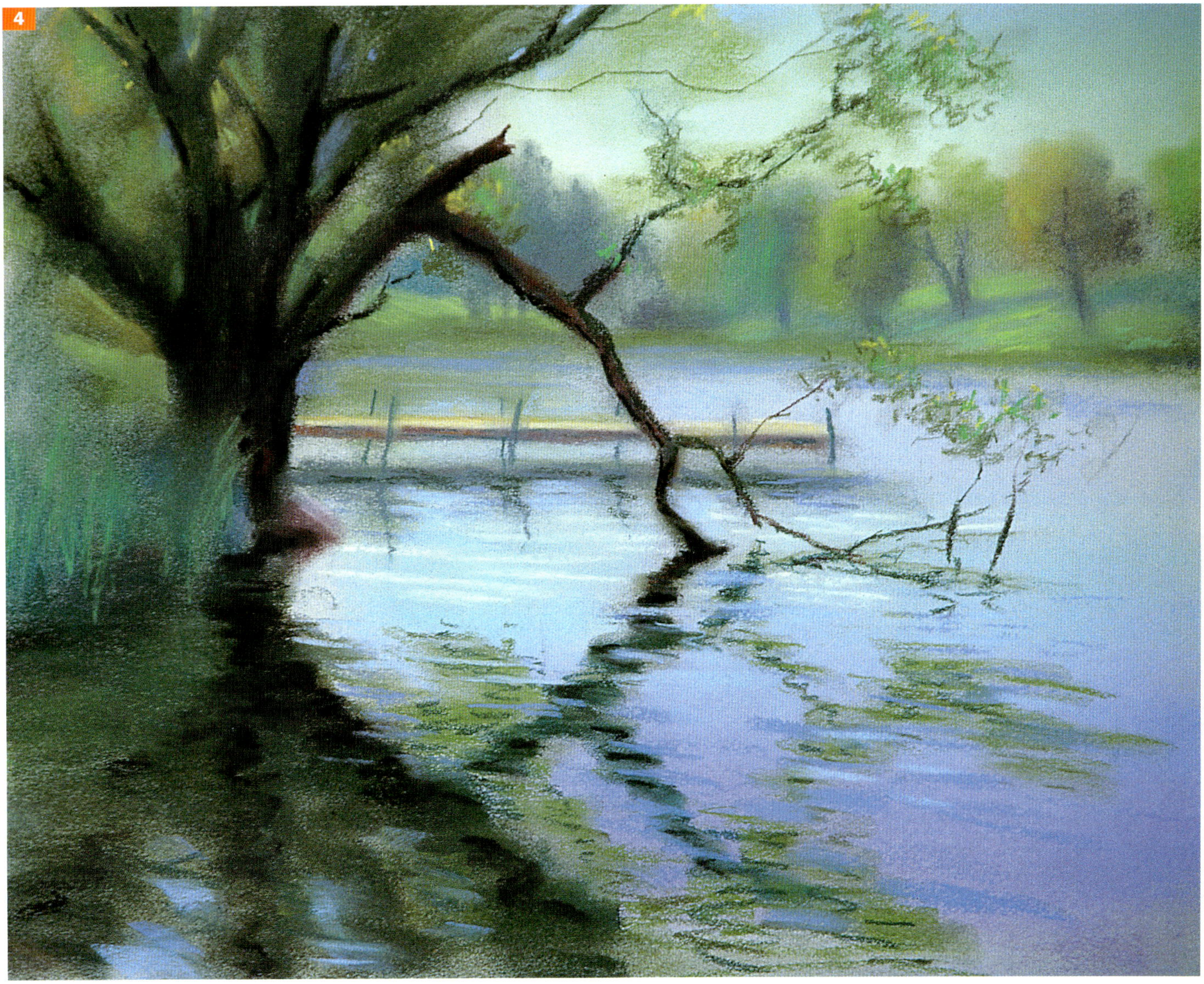

STEP FOUR To make water appear flat, it helps to somehow indicate the surface plane; the edge of the shore, the highlights, the ripples, and any floating matter can all help to create that illusion. Add more highlights to the water with light yellow deep, and place a few of the floating leaves on the surface of the water. Use dark yellow ochre on the shadowed floating leaves and gold ochre in the light areas. Next draw a thin shadow with dark Indian red below some of the leaves to deepen the shadows.

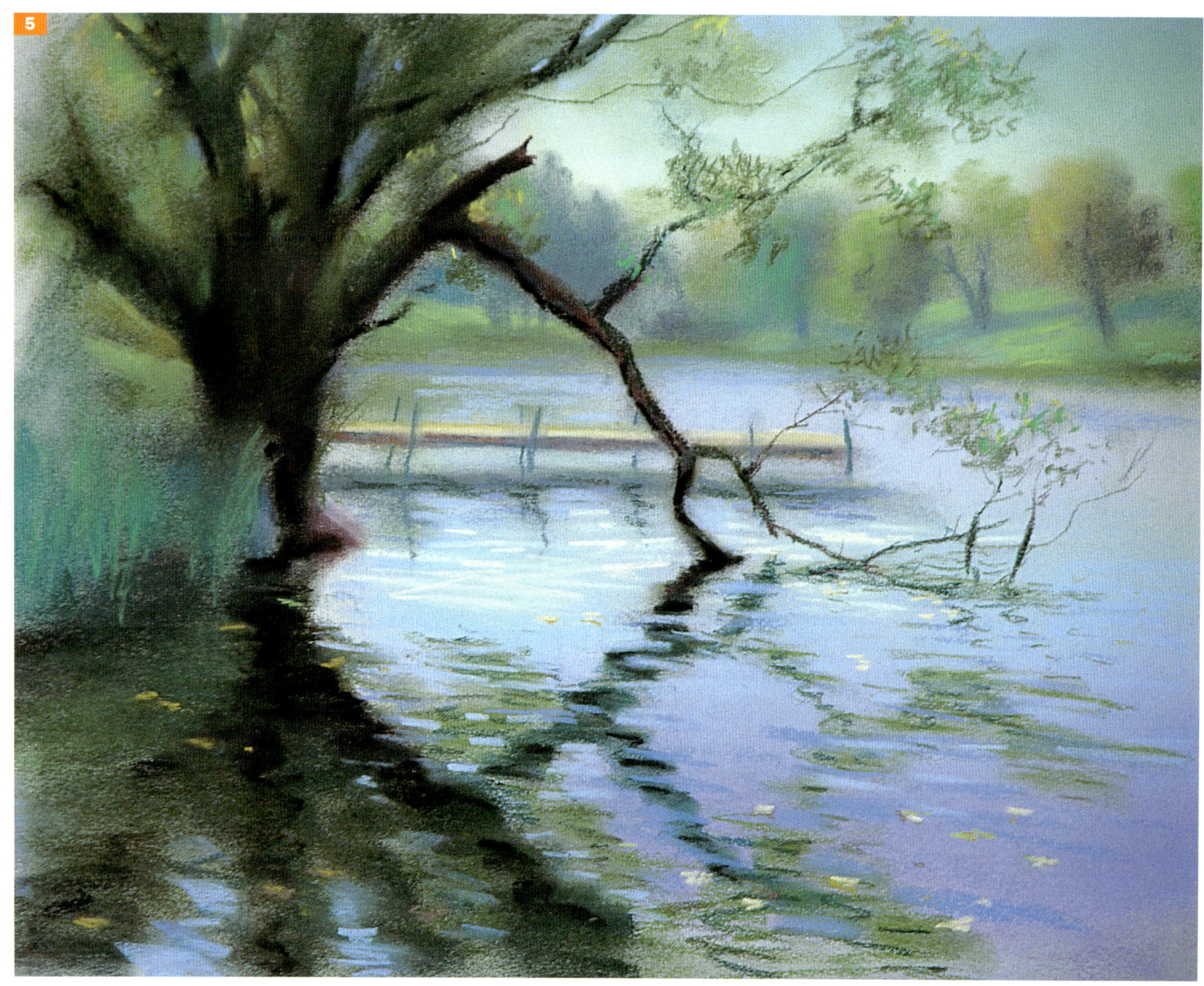

STEP FIVE For the finishing touches to your painting, add some strokes of orange in the foreground tree to indicate some backlit leaves. Finally place a few strokes of dark gold ochre to deepen the green grasses near the trunk.

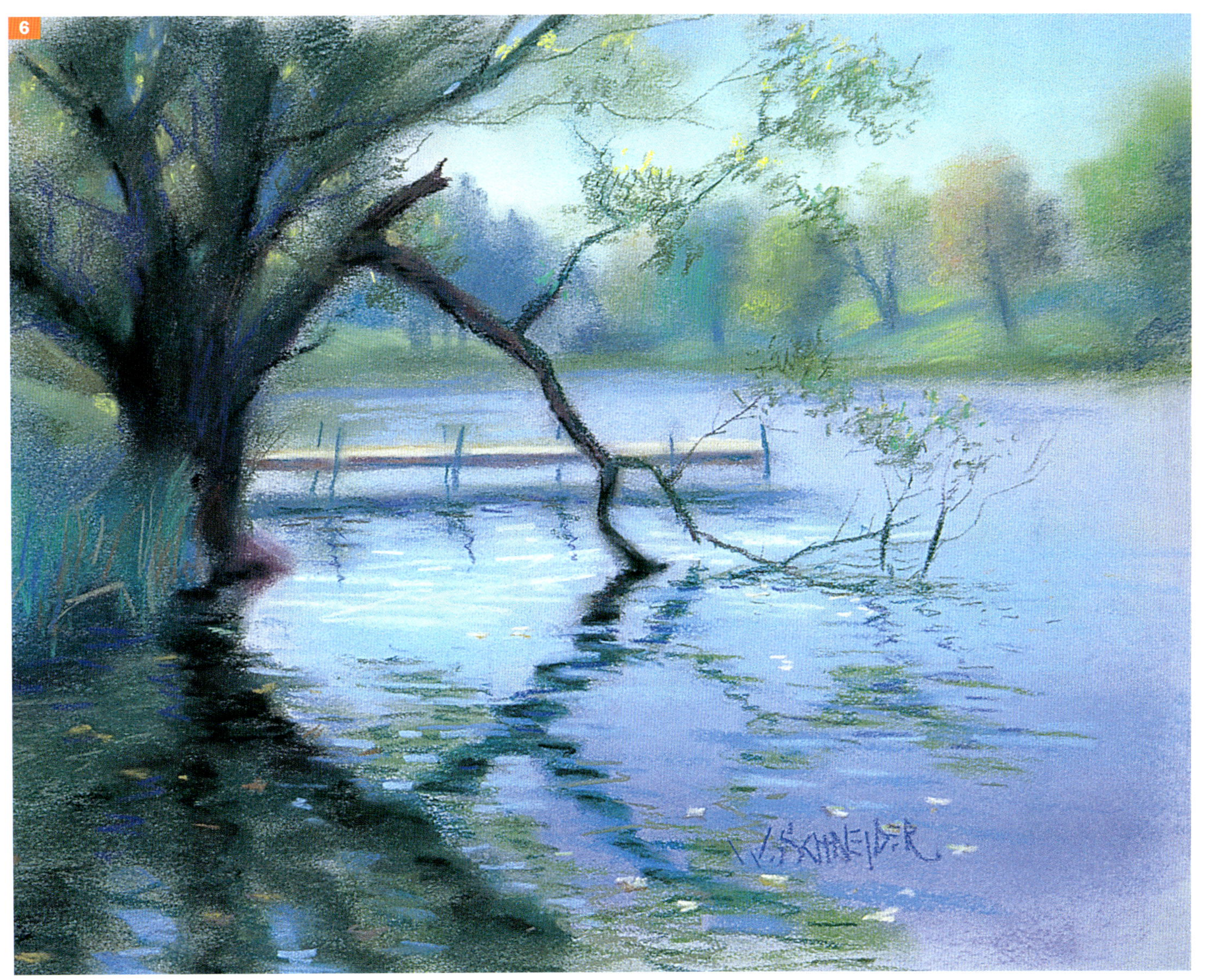

STEP SIX As you can see in the final painting, water is like a mirror—it reflects the colors in the sky as well as the colors of nearby objects. Notice that the lightest area of the water seems farther away (reflecting the horizon) and the closer water is darker. (See Lesson Five for more on creating a sense of depth.)

Lesson Three: Portrait

When you work on colored paper, the support becomes an integral part of the painting, instead of just a surface to be covered with pastel. Unless the color is applied very heavily, the pigment sits on top of the raised grain, allowing the paper to show through the strokes. Therefore the paper you choose can either set the overall tone for the painting—light, medium, or dark—or provide a warm or cool color contrast. The color of the paper can also be used to either add weight and depth to your painting, stand in for a dominant color, harmonize with the palette, or provide a contrasting tone. You can also choose a colored ground that will serve as a middle value and remain uncovered, so that all you need to paint are the light and dark values. For this portrait, the artist uses a warm burgundy paper as the base color to complement and mingle with the warm reds and yellows in the shadows, beautifully offsetting the cool, reflected light on the face. And by letting the paper stand in for some of the color, the artist was able to keep the background loosely painted, maintaining the focus on the subject.

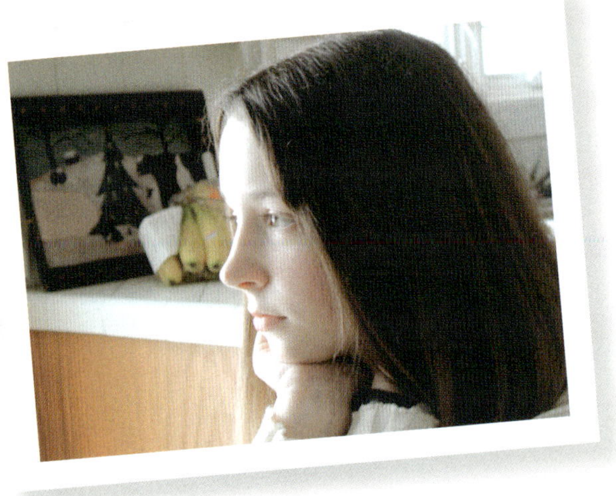

CANDID PHOTOS **It's best to paint from life; our eyes see color, value, and edges much more accurately than a photo can reproduce them. But a camera can be useful for capturing fleeting expressions, and sometimes the best portraits are of candid, unposed subjects. Try to keep a camera handy for whenever inspiration strikes!**

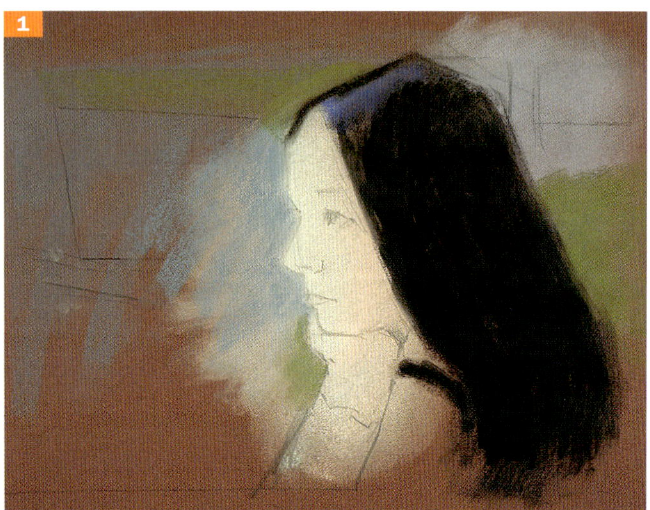

STEP ONE First apply a thin, pale base tone of light alizarin crimson with a layer of light phthalo green around the facial area. Then draw in her features over the base colors. Next establish the darkest dark (the shadow areas of her hair and her sweater) with black. Dip a soft brush in some denatured alcohol, and paint the dark pigment thoroughly into the tooth of the paper. Then place ultramarine blue for the highlight in her hair. Next establish some of the background colors with olive green and blue-gray.

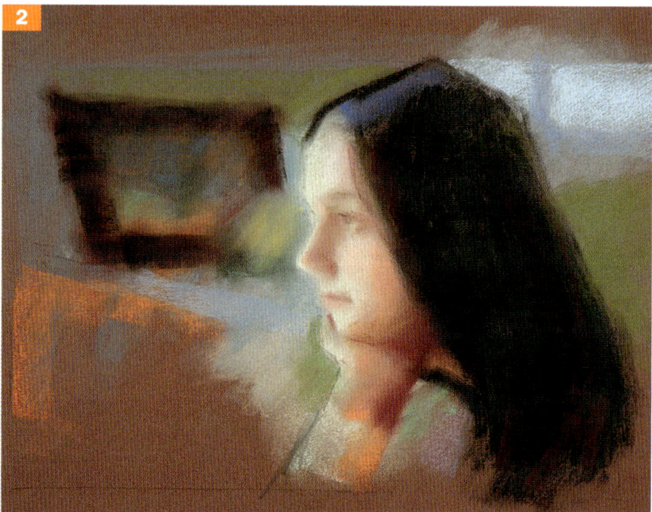

STEP TWO Use dark Indian red for the deepest shadows under her chin and a lighter value of the same color for the paler shadows on the side of her nose and around her eye. For the *halftone* (middle value) on her cheek, use light carmine, blending all the colors with your fingers. Then add dark vermilion for the deeper shadow in her hair. Next block in the brown rectangular shape on the left side with dark burnt umber. Suggest the window with light mouse gray and light cobalt blue, and add warm orange strokes of burnt sienna to the foreground.

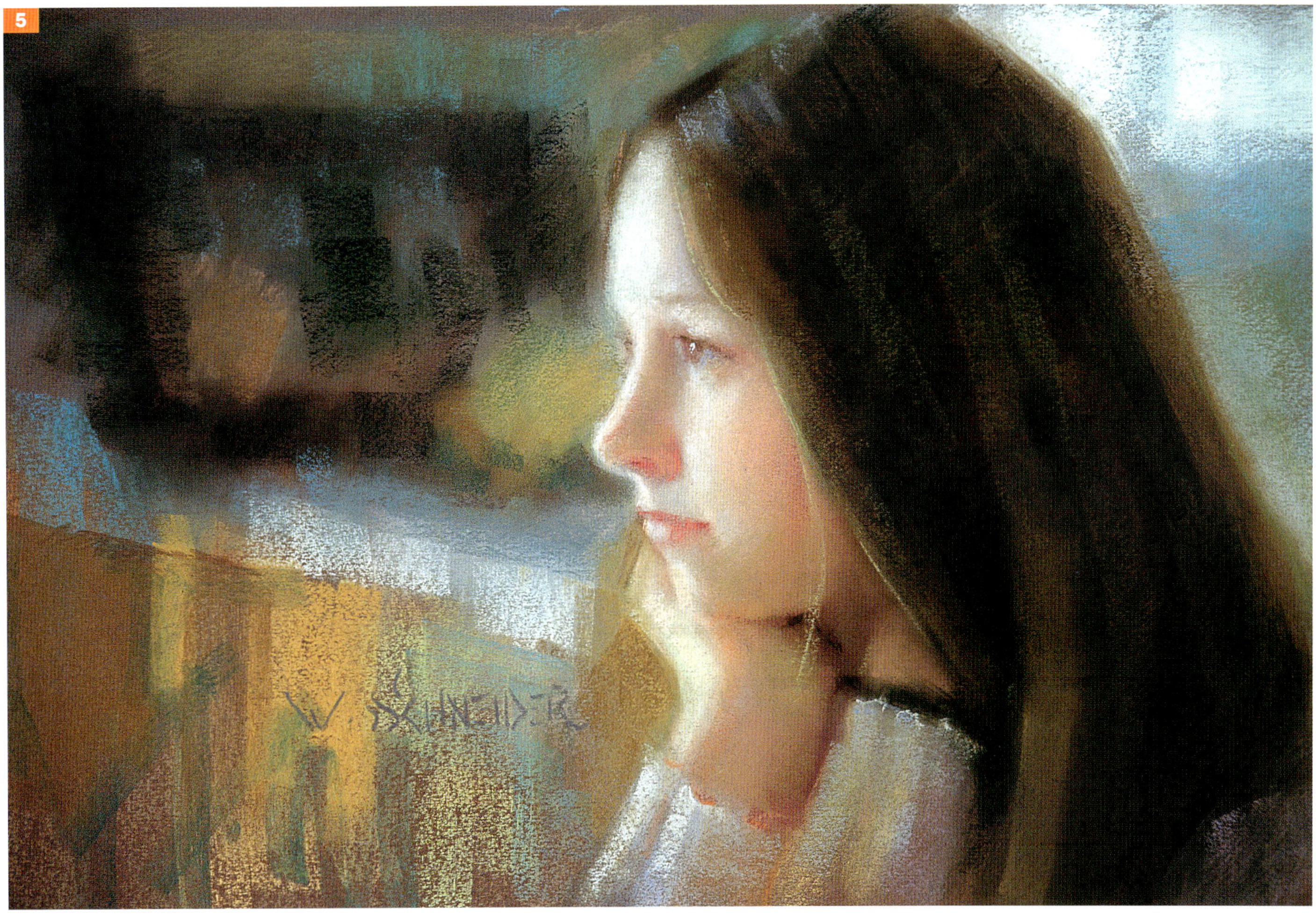

STEP FIVE Use dark burgundy for the deep tones under her chin and in the corner of her mouth; then place dark umber in her hair. Add a highlight in her eye with very light turquoise blue. Opposite and below the highlight, place a touch of chrome green. Add very light chrome green for the highlight on her nose, and use light orange and light olive green to show the light in her hair. Finally add a light red-violet deep highlight on her lower lip.

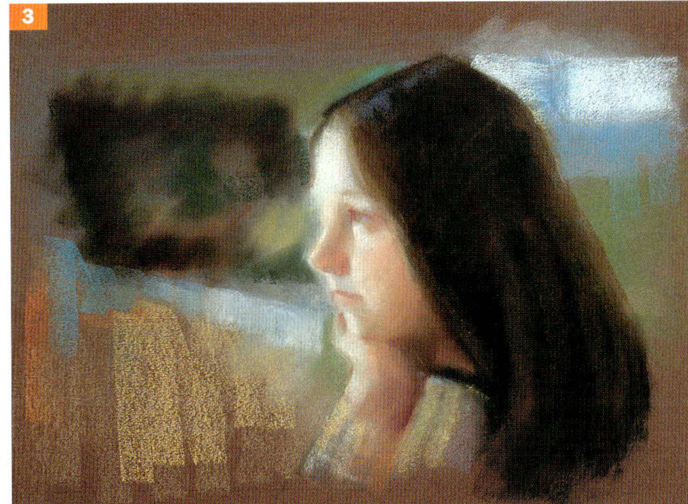

STEP THREE Next work on the halftones by applying alternating layers of light carmine red and light olive green. On the lower third of her face, use the same colors in a medium value. Use the side of your finger to blend virtually every stroke. Then cool the shadow under her chin with dark olive green, and use Indian red for the shadows on her upper lip and in the corner of her eye. Paint her sleeve with mouse gray and blue-violet, and add light gold ochre and light phthalo green. Next begin to work dark burnt umber into her hair, and brighten the highlight on her hair with light cobalt blue.

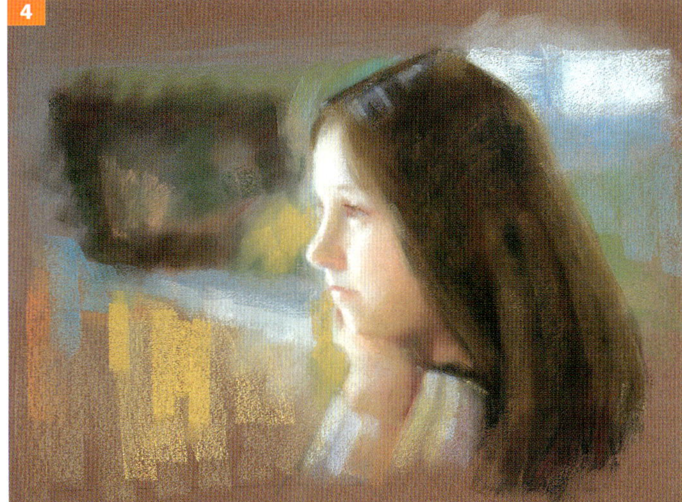

STEP FOUR Next work on the light areas of her face. Use thin layers of light permanent red and light phthalo blue for the lights in her forehead, and use light permanent red and light cobalt blue for the highlights in the middle of her face. Add the highlights in the lower third of her face with a mix of light permanent red and light chrome green. Then darken the shadow of the upper eyelid with a little black; also touch black in the center of the eye to indicate the pupil. Then work more colors into the background, with various strokes of gold ochre, reds, and greens.

Lesson Four: Street Scene

Urban street scenes can be just as captivating as more traditional landscapes. You may choose to focus on some interesting architecture, the time of day, or (as in this case) the interesting play of light and shadows on the street. Another important aspect to this composition is the *perspective:* the representation of objects in three-dimensional space to give the illusion of depth and distance. The basic rule is that objects appear to get smaller as they recede toward the *horizon line* (the actual horizon or the horizontal line level with the viewer's eye), and the spot where they seem to disappear is call the "vanishing point" (labeled VP). This lesson demonstrates the principle of *two-point perspective,* in which the two sides of a building recede along two imaginary extension lines (A and B in the diagram at right) toward two different vanishing points. (For more information, see *Perspective* in Walter Foster's Artist's Library Series.)

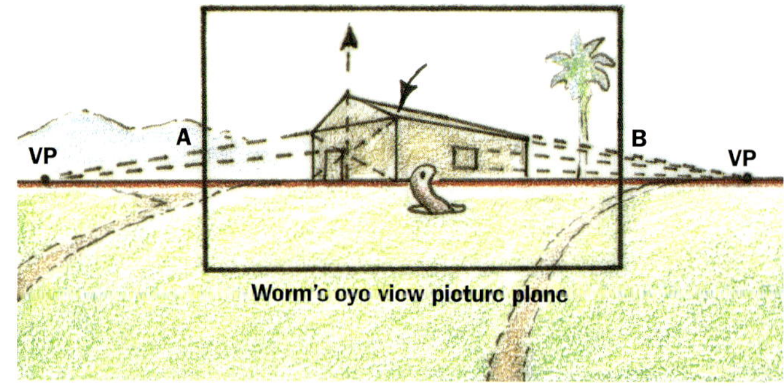

PLACING THE HORIZON LINE **Where the horizon line is placed will determine whether you're looking at the subject from above ("bird's-eye view") or below ("worm's-eye view"), as shown here. And how far apart the vanishing points are will determine how much of a building's sides are visible: the farther apart the points are, the more we see of the sides. Note that the vanishing points won't always be placed inside the picture plane. More likely, one or both will fall outside the picture plane to keep the perspective from becoming distorted.**

STEP ONE First lightly sketch the scene with vine charcoal, emphasizing the worm's-eye view by making all the houses seem tall—bring them almost to the top edge of the picture plane. By placing the buildings in the top third of the picture, the curving road gains importance and stands out as a main area of interest.

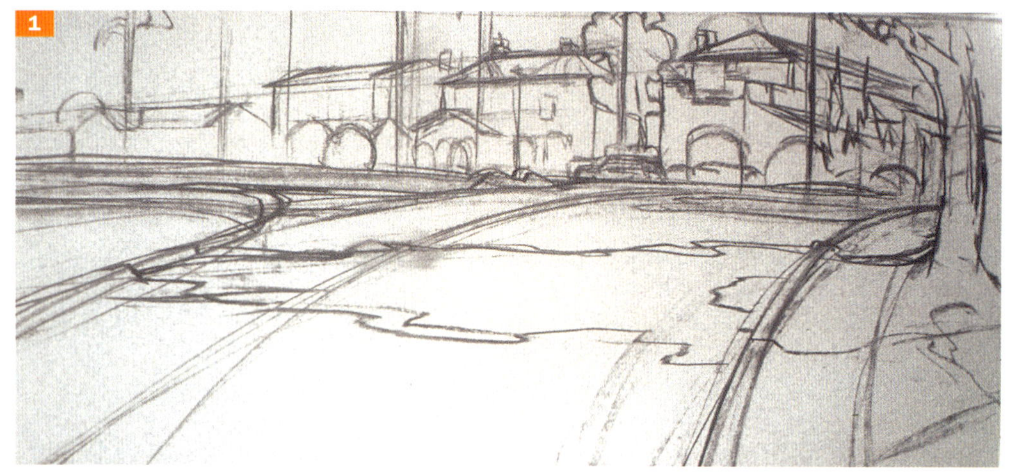

STEP TWO Carefully lay in as much color as you can, correctly placing the extremes of both value and chroma. Notice that where the dark shadow passes over the yellow line—which is lighter than the road—the shadow is also lighter. Also be sure to create a sharp contrast where the light sides of the white buildings meet the shadow sides; the shadows themselves are mostly the gray paper with just a touch of warm, reflected light from the ground.

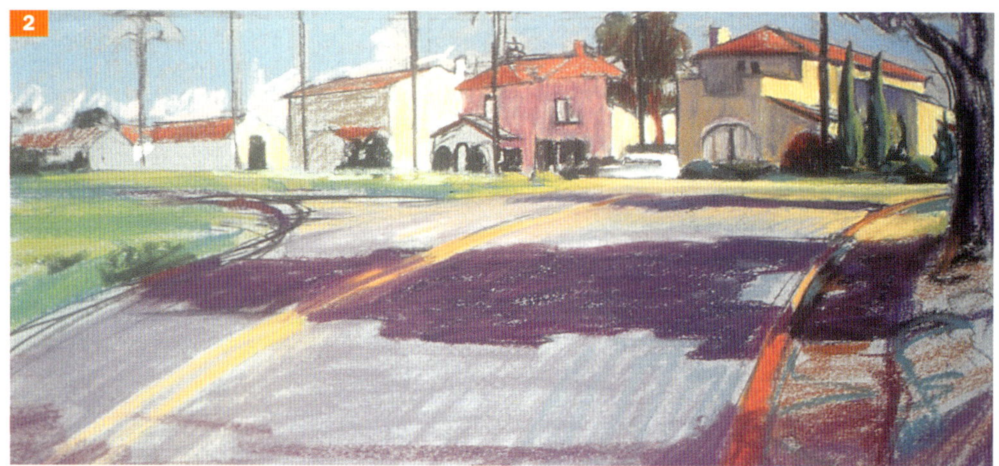

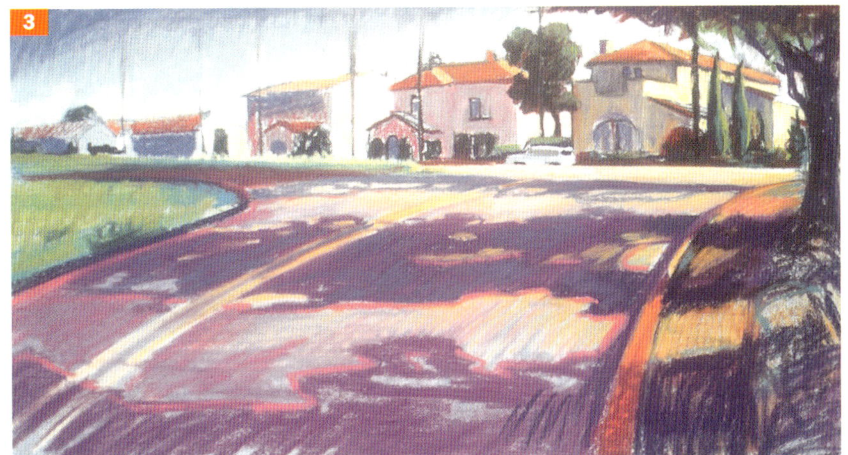

STEP THREE Now look for individual differences in all the homes, including these details and enough variation in each to counterbalance the foreground. Then develop the forms of the shadows in the street with various mixes of violets and purples.

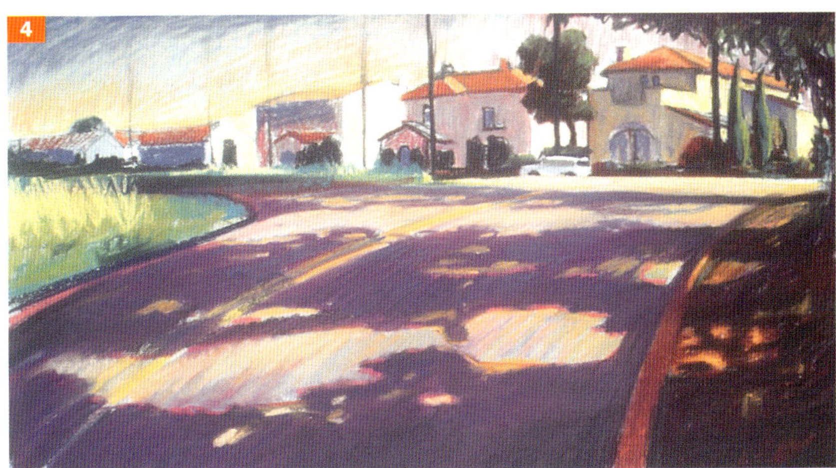

STEP FOUR Next darken and simplify the foreground so that its details do not compete with the background. To do this, smear dark umbers and violets into the lower shadow. Then cross-hatch yellows, violets, pinks, and grays into the light pavement between the shadows, leaving carmine in the shadow edges to soften the color transition.

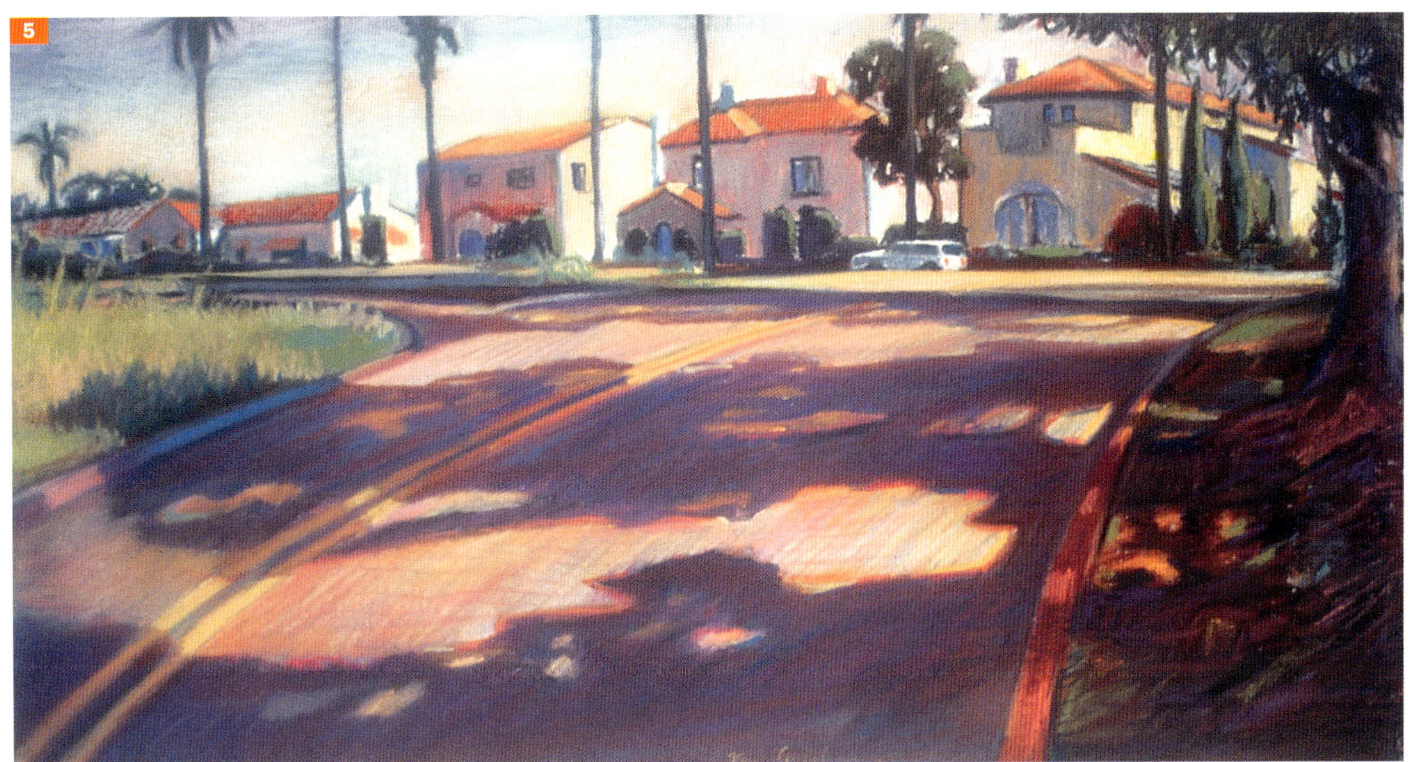

STEP FIVE Now *scumble* by lightly dragging orange and green pastels over the ground area to indicate some roots and moss on the earth. Then apply cross-hatched strokes on the road and scumble a little blue-gray into the shadow sides of the homes to show some sky reflections. Next accent the car to help the yellow lines in the road lead your eye in. As you paint, keep in mind that the street values change as the shadow passes from the right curb to the other side of the street.

Lesson Five: Landscape

Pastel's versatility makes it ideal for many artistic styles, from detailed, photo-realistic work to loose, impressionistic paintings—and it is especially well-suited for capturing the depth and vibrant colors of a beautiful landscape. In this inspiring outdoor scene, the artist conveys a realistic sense of depth in a variety of ways, as demonstrated in the sketches below. One method is to overlap elements. When one object covers part of another object (such a the tree in front of a house), the object that is overlapped—regardless of its size—will always appear to be more distant. Another technique for creating depth is *aerial perspective:* the tendency of objects to appear grayer and less detailed as they recede into the distance. Notice that the soft edges and lack of detail in the houses in this painting make them appear to be farther away. And light-colored objects appear slightly darker as they recede, whereas dark-colored objects appear lighter.

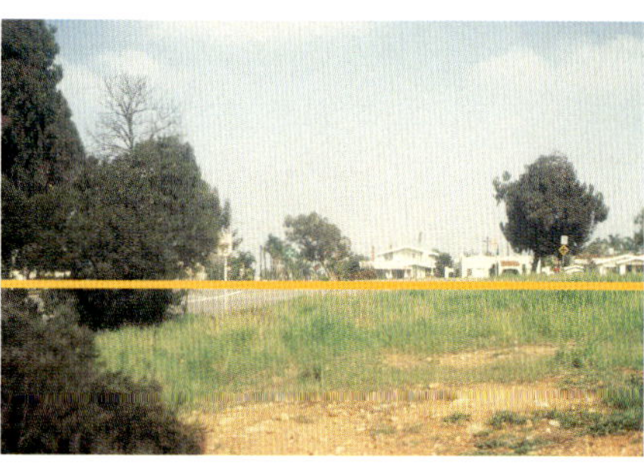

CONVEYING DEPTH **The horizon line provides another visual cue to depth: The closer an object is to the level of the horizon, the farther away the object seems to be.**

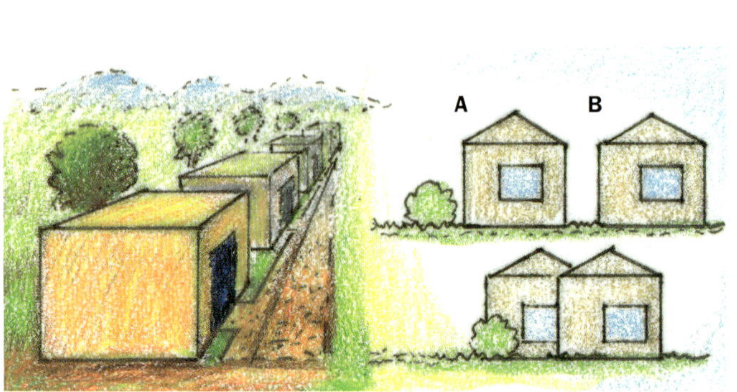

USING AERIAL PERSPECTIVE **As the light orange box recedes, it gets grayer and slightly darker, while its dark door and the trees get gradually paler.**

OVERLAPPING **Houses A and B are the same size, but when B overlaps A, it seems to be in front of A—without any change in its color or dimension.**

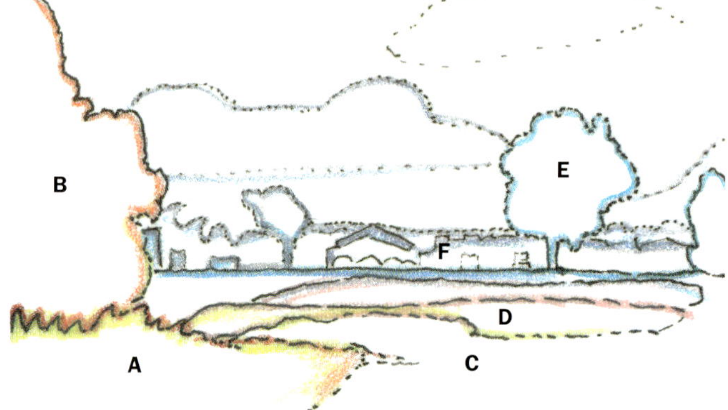

CREATING DEPTH **This diagram shows how overlapping is used to create depth in this lesson. For example, plane A makes the dark tree B seem to be a bit farther back into the picture, while area C (because of the low viewpoint) makes D appear much farther back. In addition, background tree E seems to be about one street-width away from the row of houses F.**

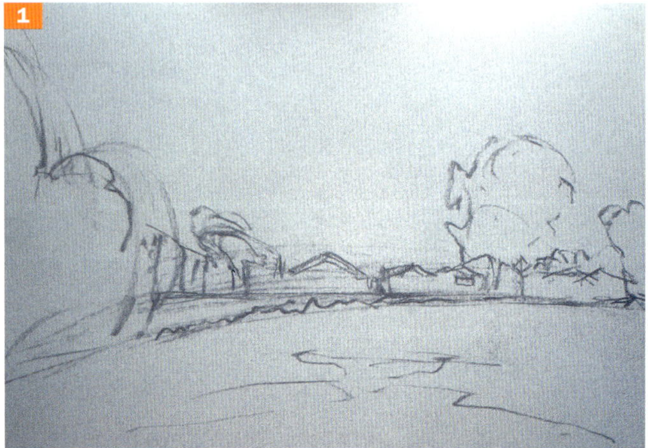

STEP ONE With vine charcoal, lightly sketch in the basic shapes of the main elements. When placing the horizon line, think about the relationship between the wide, expansive sky and the large grassy field, as well as the size of the interesting row of small, bright homes that lie in between.

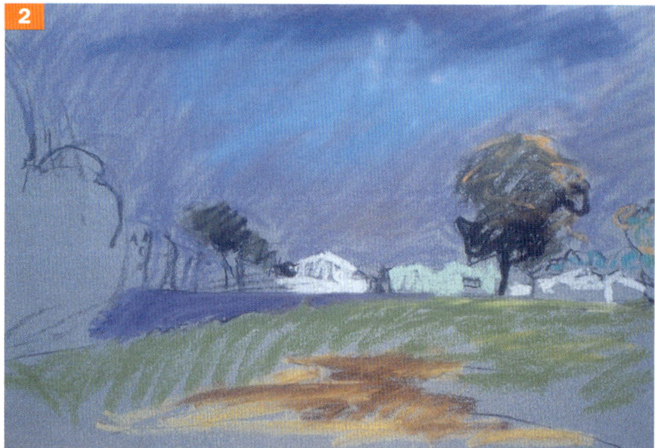

STEP TWO Next block in the general areas of color, placing the lightest light (a white house) and darkest dark (one of the trees). On the road, lay in a darker purple than necessary, since you can tone it down later if needed. Then rub orange into black to create the dark, rich green on the trees.

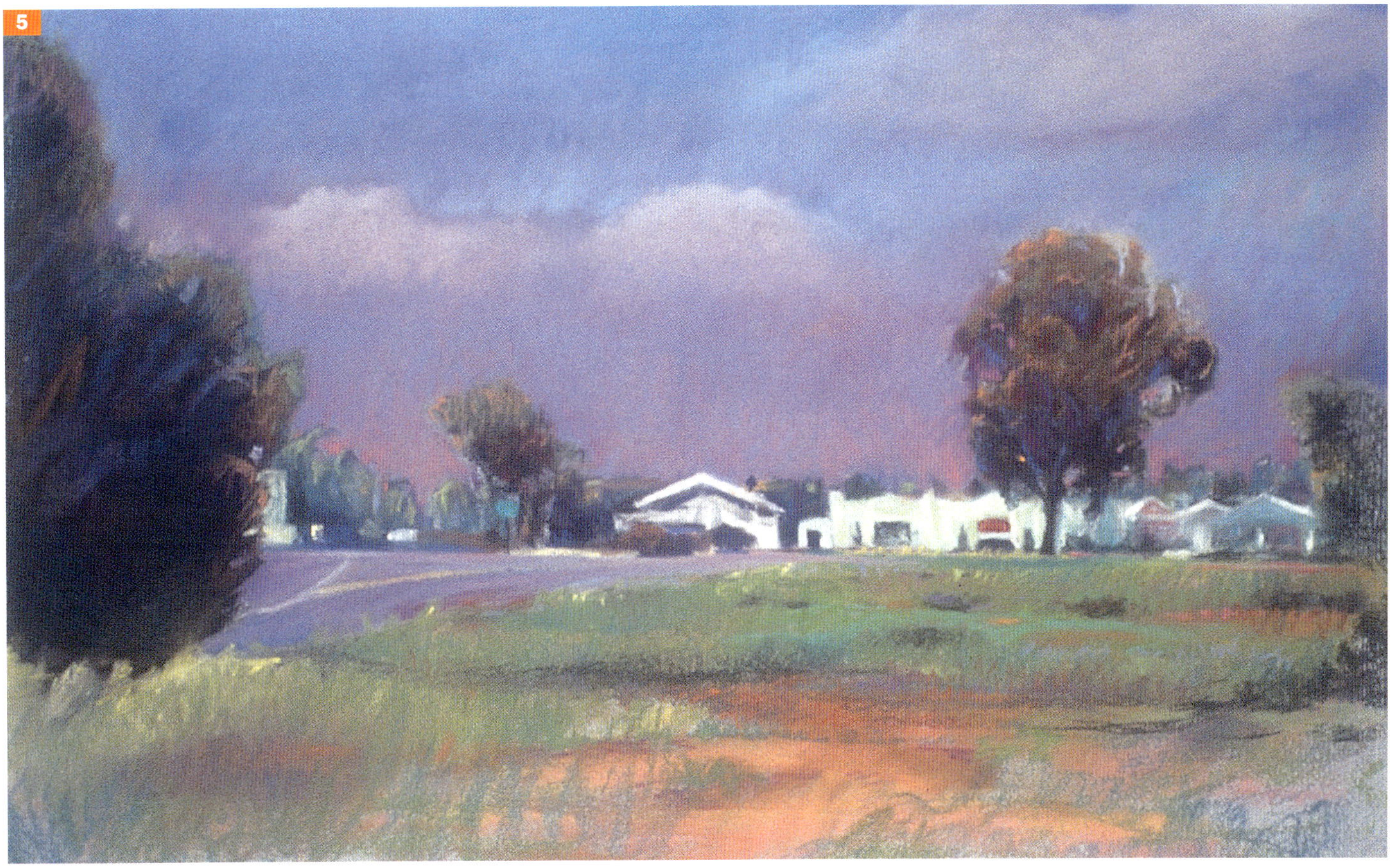

STEP FIVE Now add a third dark shrub on the right side to balance the composition. For the final overlapping strokes in the field, make the edges crisper and add dark accents. Scumble a little deep blue into the trees, and use a little darker blue-green to tone down the homes on the right side, keeping the attention on the other side of the tree.

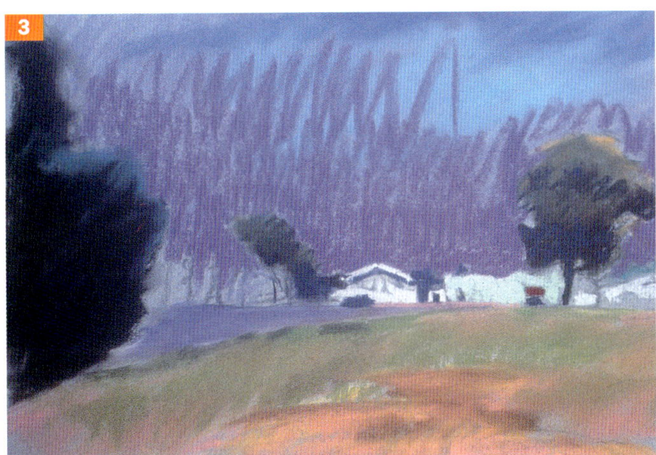

STEP THREE Next give the purple sky a deeper value, which makes the houses seem to glow. Then lay in a light blue-green color on all but one of the houses. Make the foreground tree darker by rubbing on mixes of black, viridian green, and purple. And to help unify the field with the sky, add some pink to the greens and browns, blending with your finger.

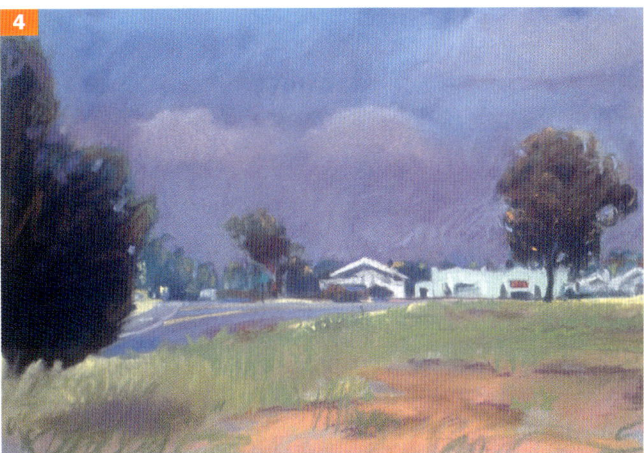

STEP FOUR Use your finger to blend the purple horizon into the sky, and paint some white clouds to repeat the horizontal curves of the field. Add orange strokes to the trees, and lighten the road at the top. Then place dark, scruffy green strokes in the field to create subtle overlapping planes, and paint some dark trees behind the homes to make them even brighter.

Lesson Six: Self-Portrait

You may be the most dependable model you will ever have. You are always on time, no hour is too early or too late, and there is no limit to the number of expressions you can make. And, when armed with a mirror, painting self-portraits gives you the luxury of experimenting with many angles and poses that a model might not care to hold. You can try drawing your head in various positions, using a second or third mirror for profiles, or practice painting under natural light during the day and under spot or fluorescent lights at night.

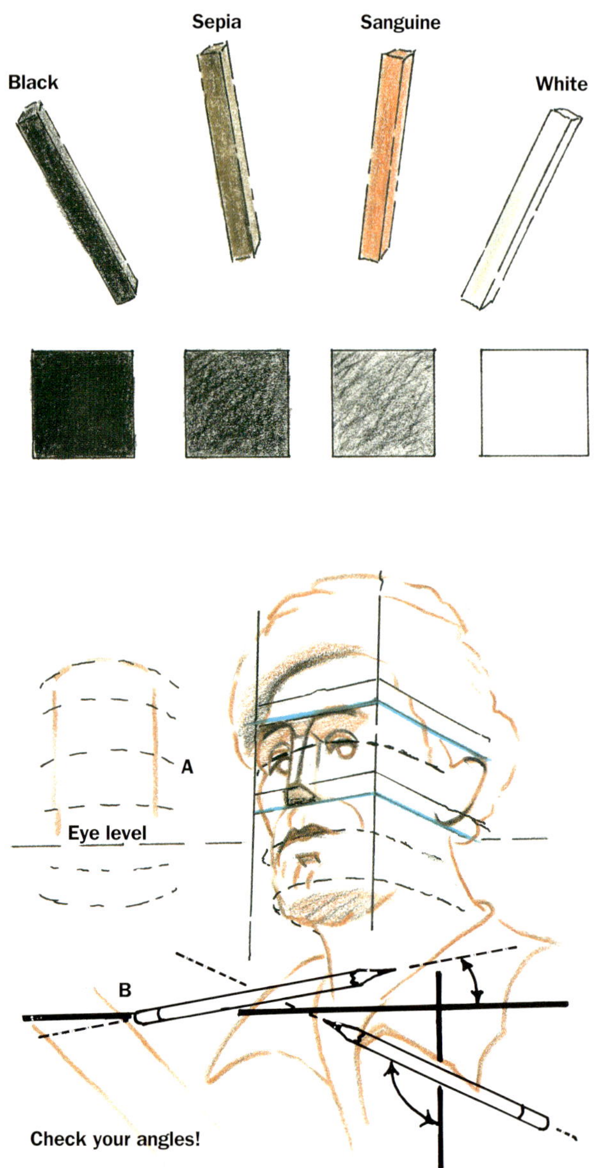

APPLYING PERSPECTIVE IN PORTRAITS **This diagram shows how to use correct perspective when your head is tilted back and your features are seen from below. Notice that the head follows the same laws of perspective that a cube or cylinder does (A). The key to perspective is to correctly draw each angle of the forms you see in relation to horizontal and vertical axes (B). Then use your pencil to check these angles.**

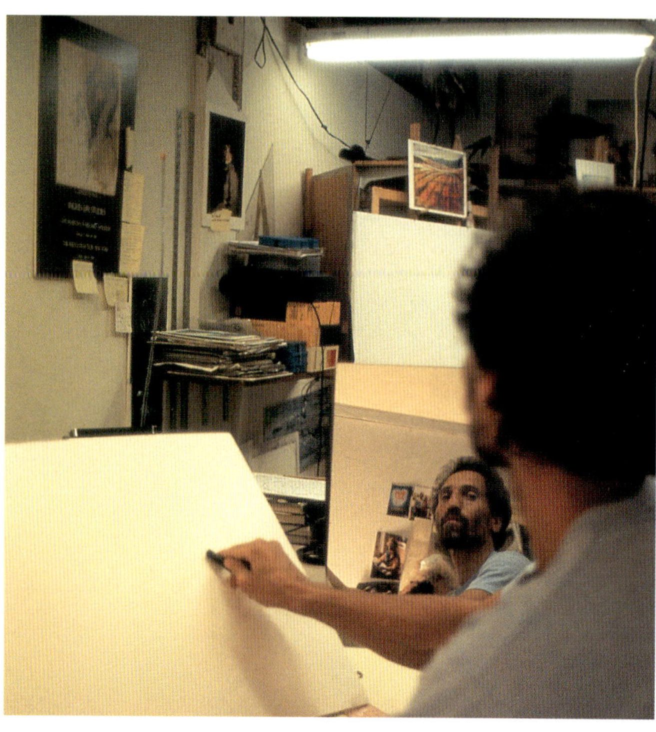

SETTING UP FOR A SELF-PORTRAIT **This self-portrait setup utilizes fluorescent light, and the mirror provides a constant source of reference.**

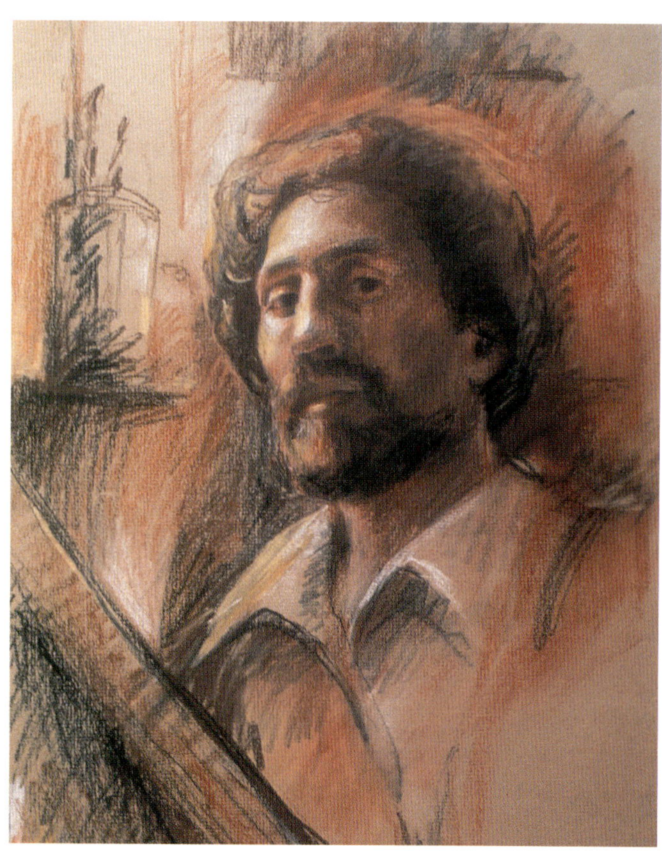

USING LIMITED COLORS **A midtone grayish paper and a limited palette of pastel colors (black, sepia, sanguine, and white) produce a full range of values.**

Painting in Full Color

In this self-portrait, the yellowish tone of the hat works well with the red-violet shirt and the blue background. When painting in full color, you must first identify all the values. The best way to do this is to squint your eyes while looking at your subject. Try squinting at the two-color drawing below, and you will see that there are three main values—the background and shadows are a dark value, the shirt is a middle value, and the face is light (accented with dark values). As the lightest area, the face will come forward in the painting and will naturally become the center of interest.

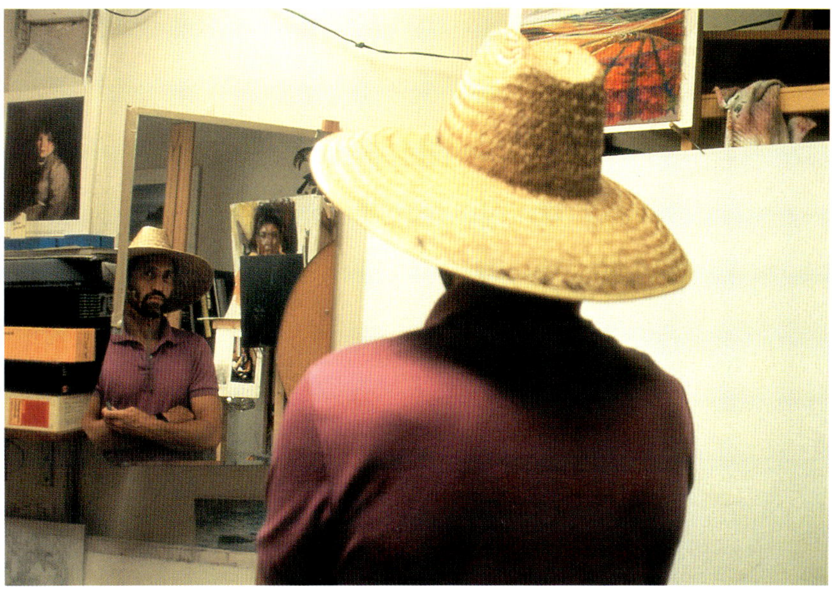

TYPICAL LIFE-SIZE SETUP **When working on a life-size self-portrait, you will need a large mirror. Here the mirror is hinged to a wall so its angle can easily be changed.**

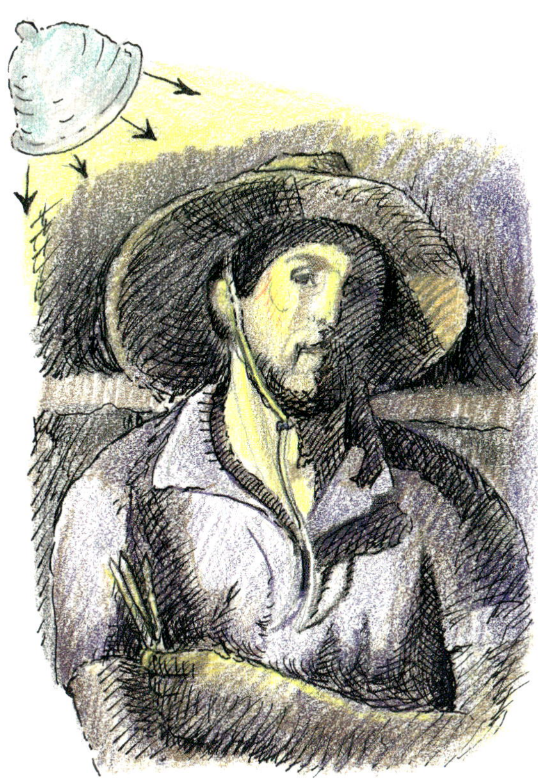

LIGHTING **For this self-portrait, the light is coming from a traditional angle—45 degrees high and off to the side. This angle accentuates the shadows and helps you see depth and volume.**

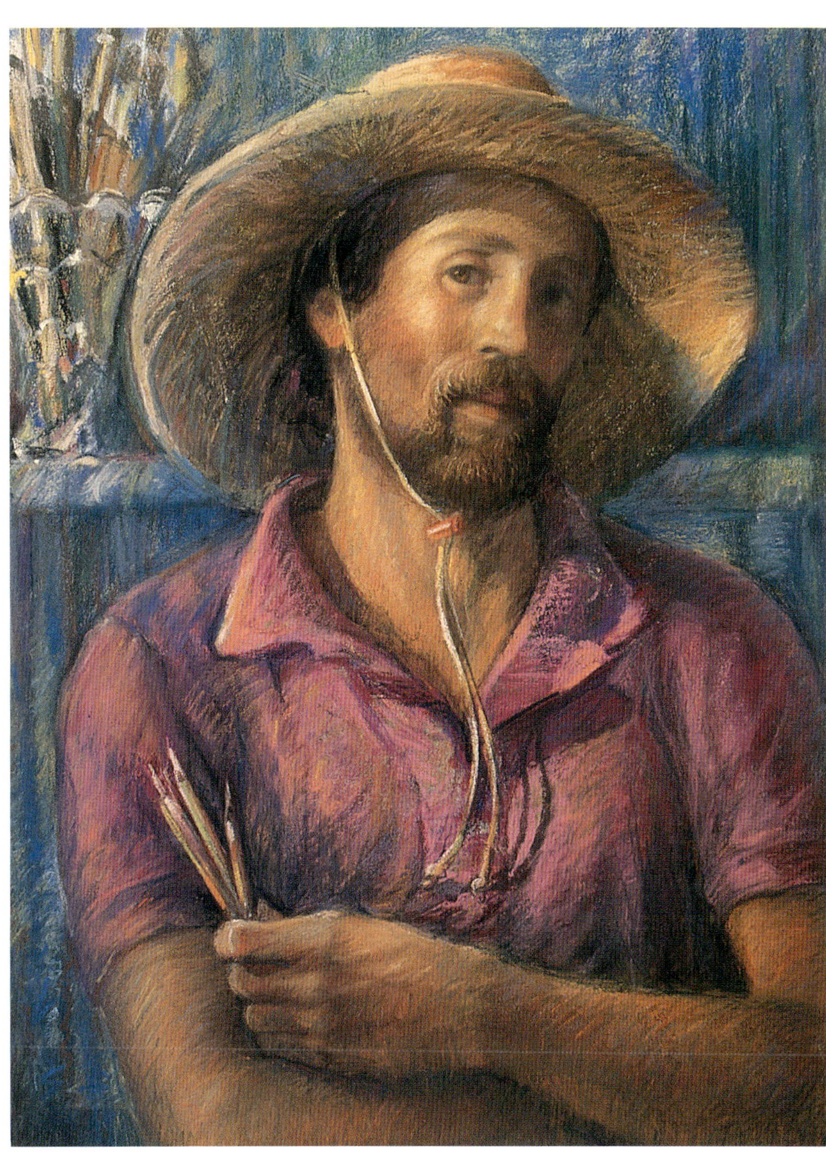

CAPTURING YOUR LIKENESS **Carefully copy all the shapes, values, and colors you see, and refine your painting with details. And remember that all skin tones are variations of red mixed with yellow-orange, plus touches of similar values of green or blue.**

Lesson Seven: Koala

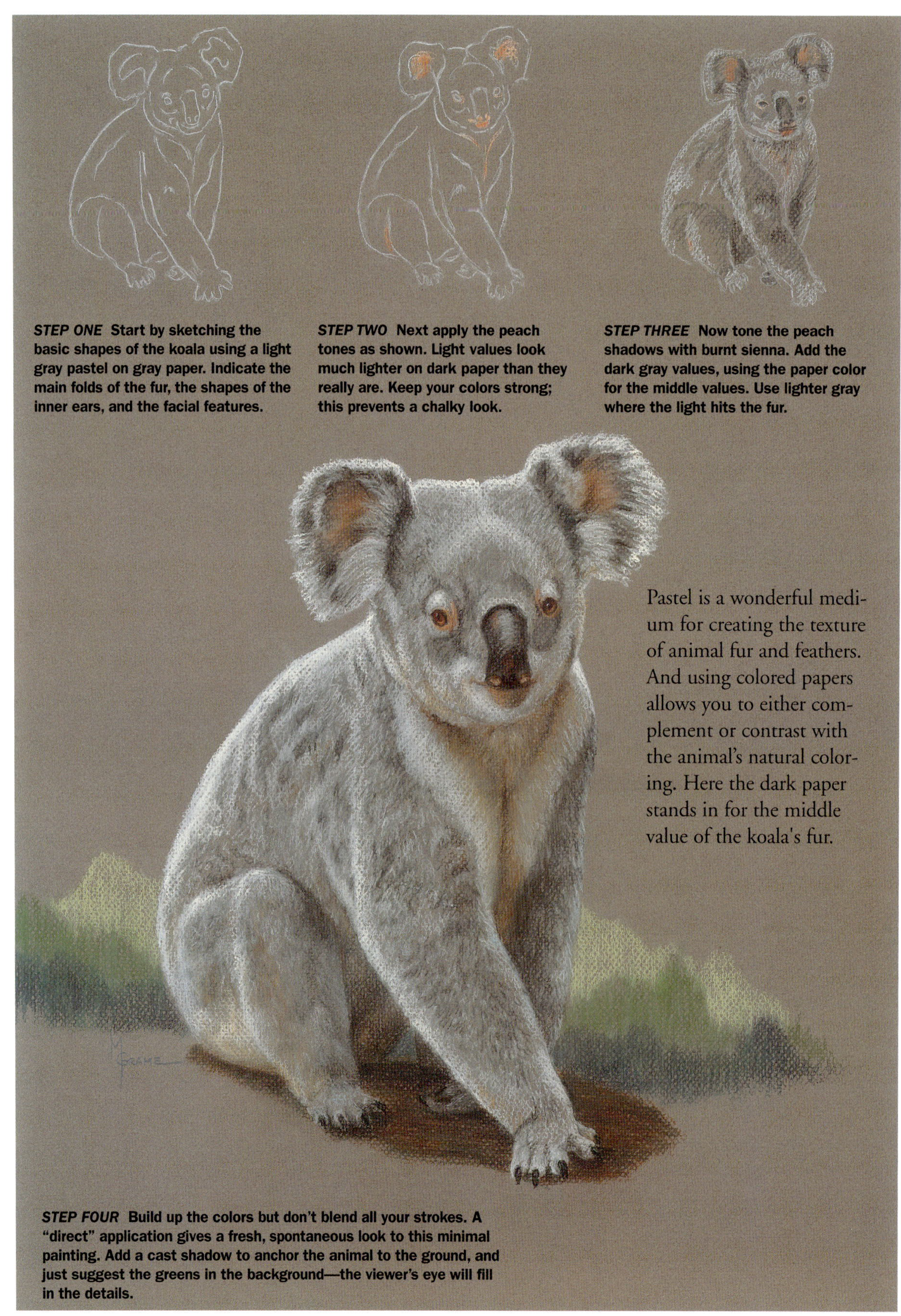

STEP ONE **Start by sketching the basic shapes of the koala using a light gray pastel on gray paper. Indicate the main folds of the fur, the shapes of the inner ears, and the facial features.**

STEP TWO **Next apply the peach tones as shown. Light values look much lighter on dark paper than they really are. Keep your colors strong; this prevents a chalky look.**

STEP THREE **Now tone the peach shadows with burnt sienna. Add the dark gray values, using the paper color for the middle values. Use lighter gray where the light hits the fur.**

Pastel is a wonderful medium for creating the texture of animal fur and feathers. And using colored papers allows you to either complement or contrast with the animal's natural coloring. Here the dark paper stands in for the middle value of the koala's fur.

STEP FOUR **Build up the colors but don't blend all your strokes. A "direct" application gives a fresh, spontaneous look to this minimal painting. Add a cast shadow to anchor the animal to the ground, and just suggest the greens in the background—the viewer's eye will fill in the details.**

Lesson Eight: Cockatoo

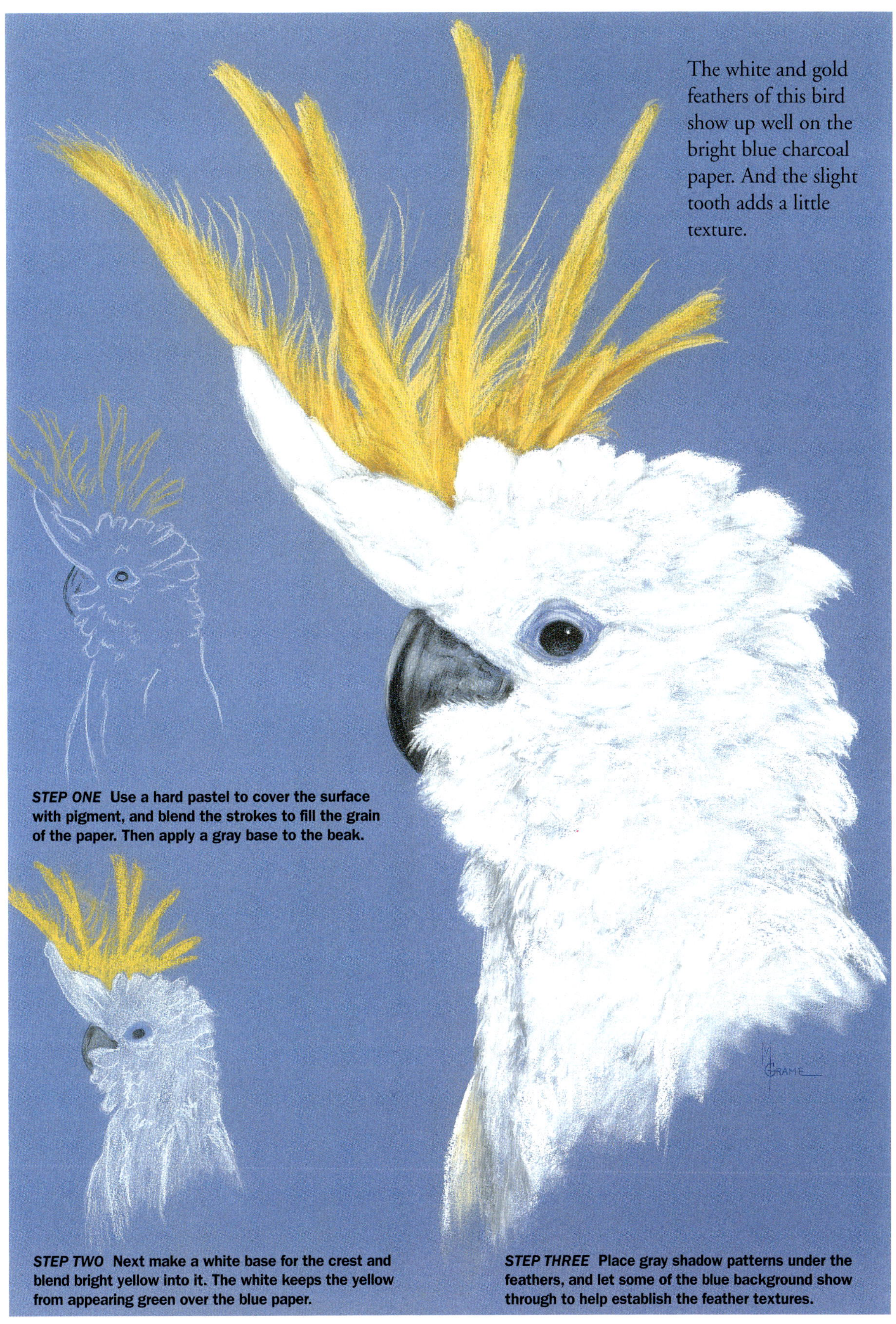

The white and gold feathers of this bird show up well on the bright blue charcoal paper. And the slight tooth adds a little texture.

STEP ONE **Use a hard pastel to cover the surface with pigment, and blend the strokes to fill the grain of the paper. Then apply a gray base to the beak.**

STEP TWO **Next make a white base for the crest and blend bright yellow into it. The white keeps the yellow from appearing green over the blue paper.**

STEP THREE **Place gray shadow patterns under the feathers, and let some of the blue background show through to help establish the feather textures.**

Lesson Nine: Cat

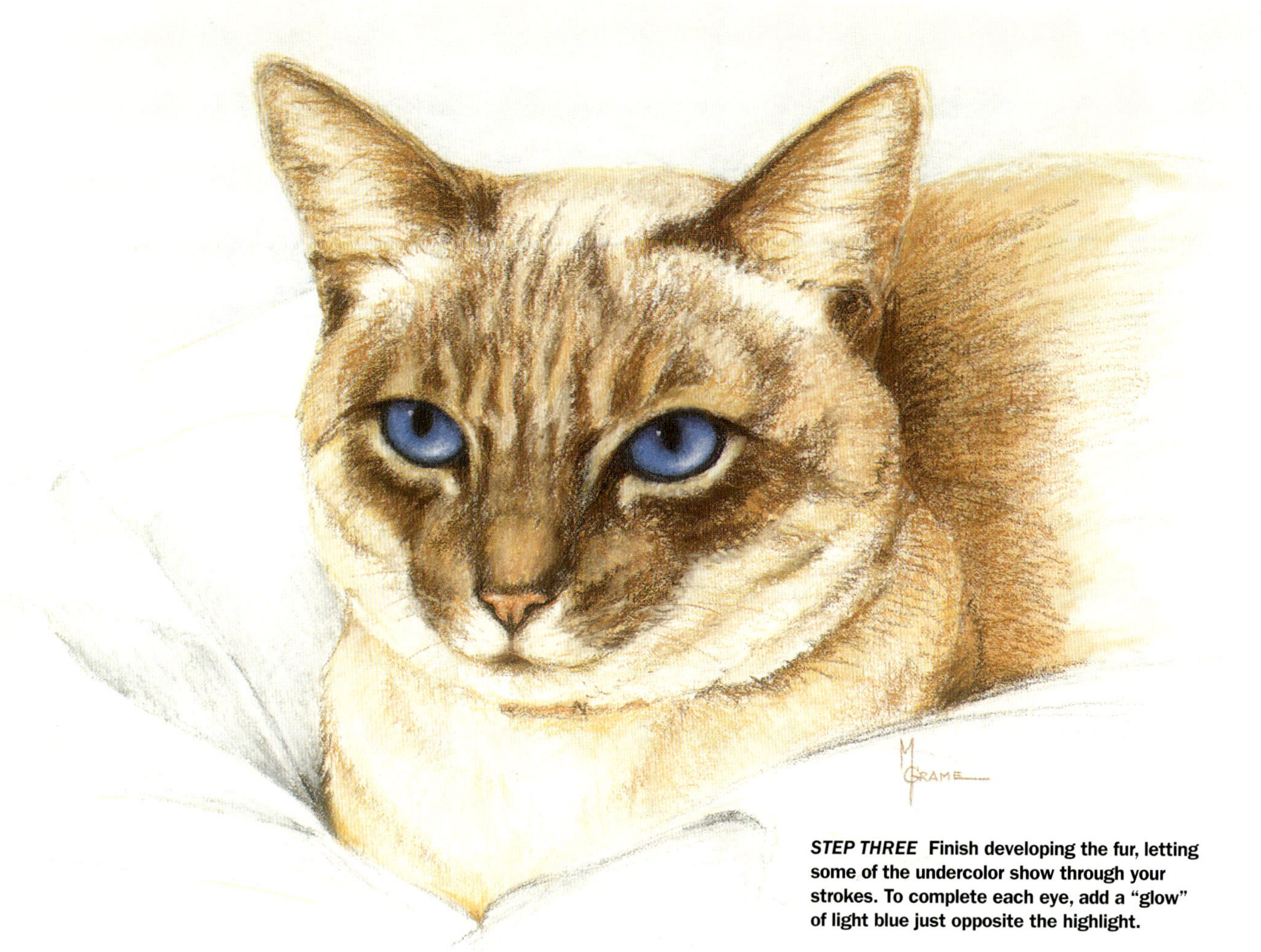

STEP THREE **Finish developing the fur, letting some of the undercolor show through your strokes. To complete each eye, add a "glow" of light blue just opposite the highlight.**

This lovely Siamese cat was done on a special pastel cloth. Because the cloth is white, you have to create the base color of the cat's fur with pastels and denatured alcohol as explained on page 12 (step one). This saves most of the tooth of the paper for subsequent applications of pastel.

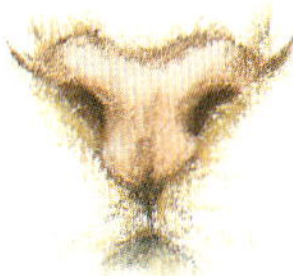

DETAIL **Render the cat's nose as a modified triangle shape, leaving the nostrils open on the sides. Tone the outer edges of the nose with a darker value of the pink.**

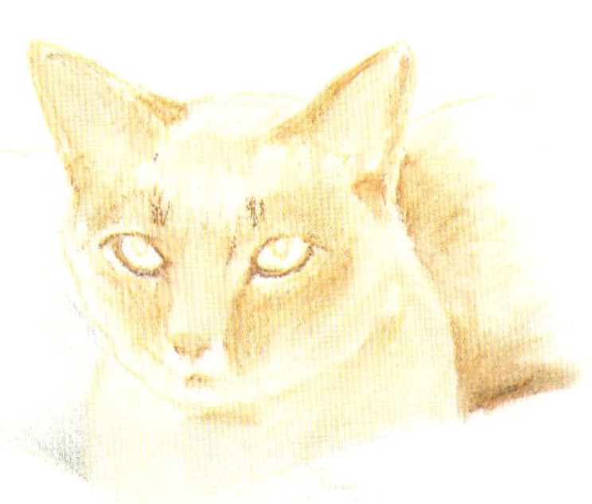

STEP ONE **Use a tan pastel pencil to draw the basic shapes. Next fill in the drawing with pastels and a brush dipped in alcohol. Allow it to dry.**

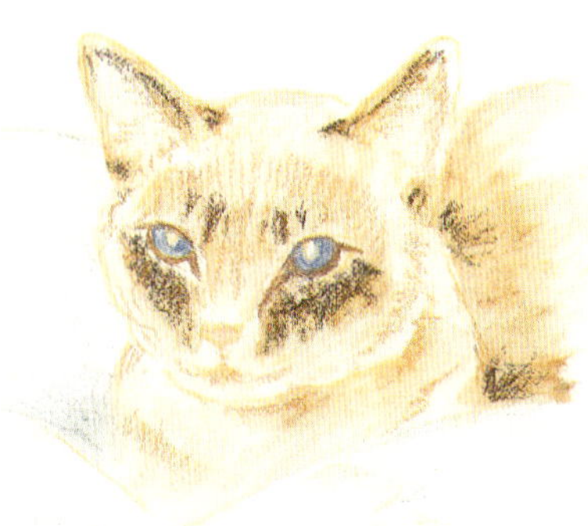

STEP TWO **Apply the darker values with dry pastel; then add the lighter hues. Use cerulean blue for the eyes, darkening them around the pupils.**

Lesson Ten: Monkey

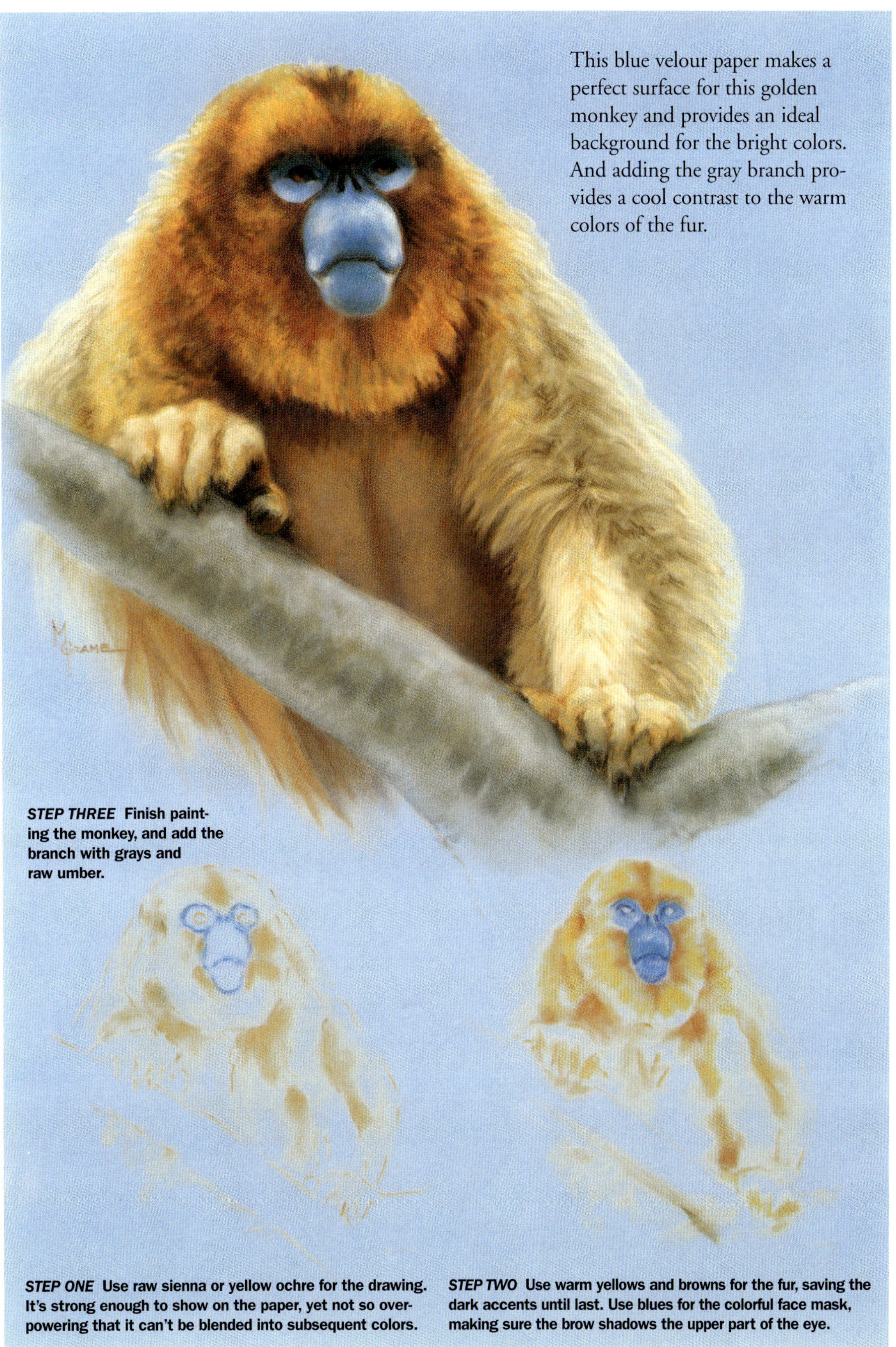

This blue velour paper makes a perfect surface for this golden monkey and provides an ideal background for the bright colors. And adding the gray branch provides a cool contrast to the warm colors of the fur.

STEP THREE **Finish painting the monkey, and add the branch with grays and raw umber.**

STEP ONE **Use raw sienna or yellow ochre for the drawing. It's strong enough to show on the paper, yet not so overpowering that it can't be blended into subsequent colors.**

STEP TWO **Use warm yellows and browns for the fur, saving the dark accents until last. Use blues for the colorful face mask, making sure the brow shadows the upper part of the eye.**

Lesson Eleven: Lion

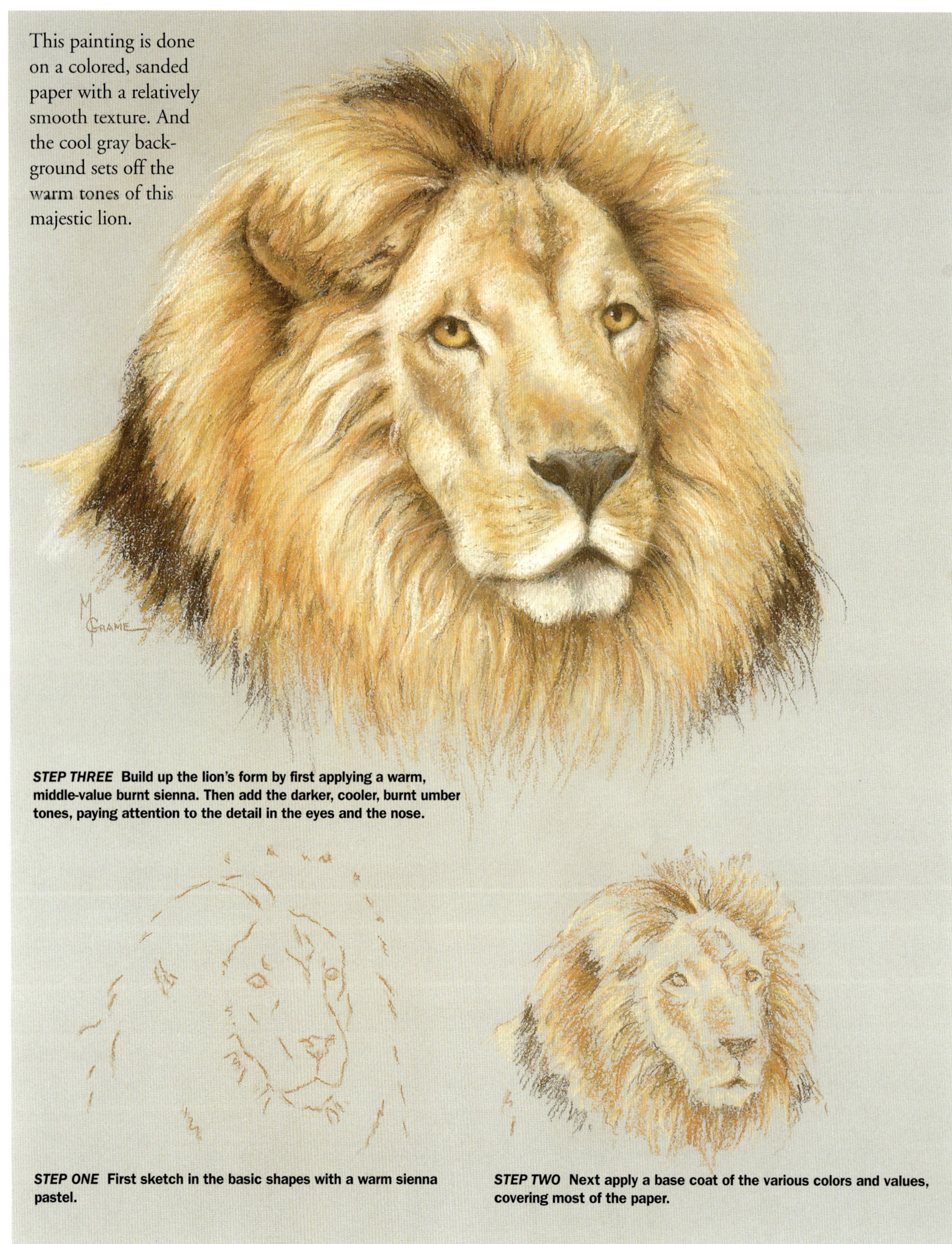

This painting is done on a colored, sanded paper with a relatively smooth texture. And the cool gray background sets off the warm tones of this majestic lion.

STEP THREE **Build up the lion's form by first applying a warm, middle-value burnt sienna. Then add the darker, cooler, burnt umber tones, paying attention to the detail in the eyes and the nose.**

STEP ONE **First sketch in the basic shapes with a warm sienna pastel.**

STEP TWO **Next apply a base coat of the various colors and values, covering most of the paper.**

Lesson Twelve: Rooster

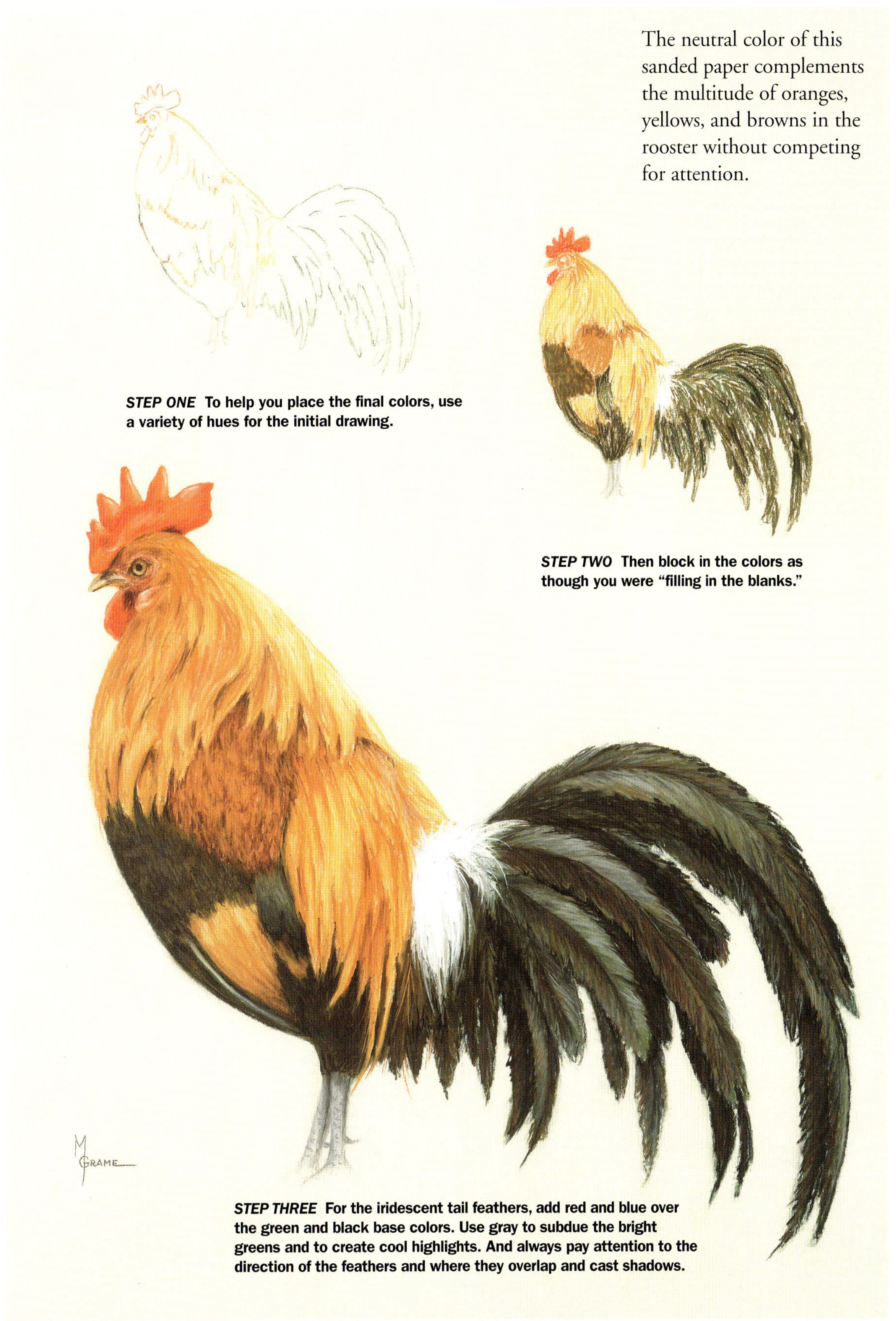

The neutral color of this sanded paper complements the multitude of oranges, yellows, and browns in the rooster without competing for attention.

STEP ONE **To help you place the final colors, use a variety of hues for the initial drawing.**

STEP TWO **Then block in the colors as though you were "filling in the blanks."**

STEP THREE **For the iridescent tail feathers, add red and blue over the green and black base colors. Use gray to subdue the bright greens and to create cool highlights. And always pay attention to the direction of the feathers and where they overlap and cast shadows.**

Conclusion

Pastel is a wonderfully versatile medium. As you become familiar with it, you will discover even more interesting effects and techniques to use in your paintings. Just remember to practice and experiment, and you will soon become truly skilled with this medium. And making mistakes is part of the learning process, so don't be afraid to try new things!

What you achieve with your pastels depends on how you choose to use them. Try painting on different surfaces, textures, and colors of paper. If you keep an open mind, you'll soon discover your own unique approach. For the most successful paintings, study your subjects, and then decide what approach truly inspires you. We hope you have learned many ways to create beautiful art through the lessons in this book. Enjoy your new-found skills!

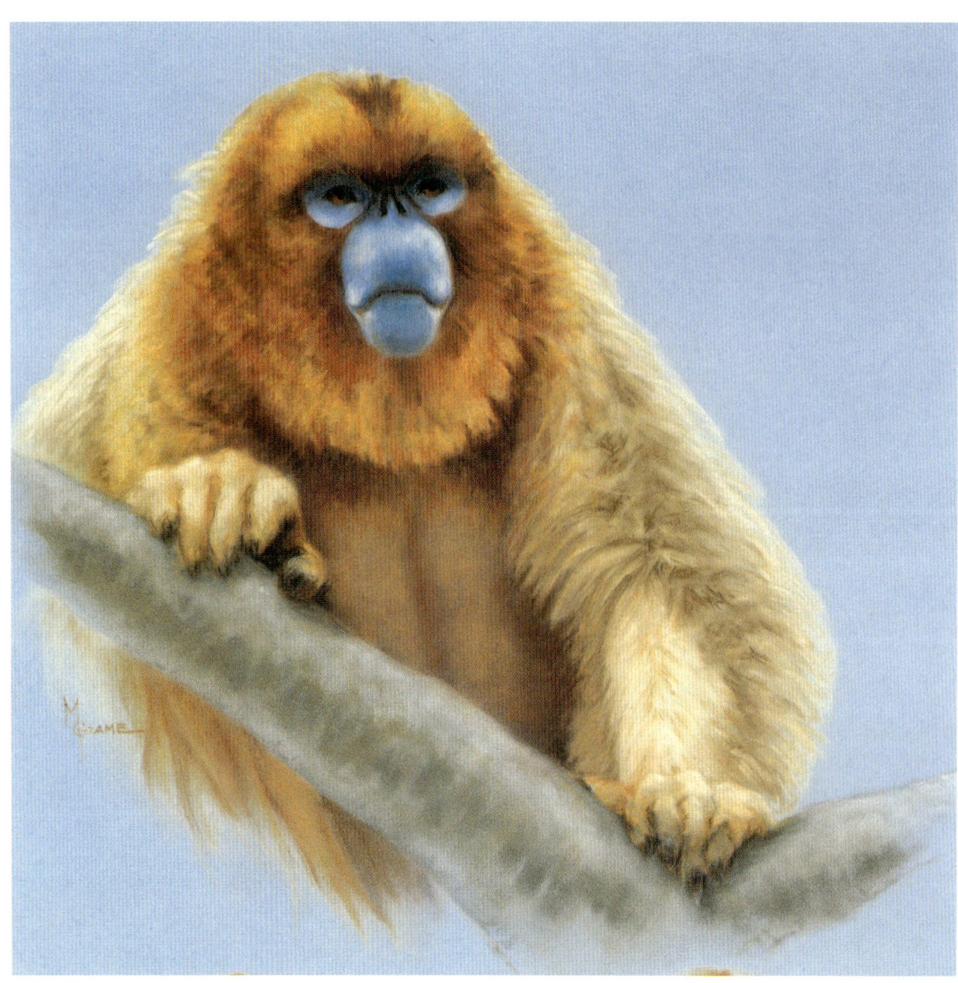